AROUND bOston WITH KIDS

by Lisa Oppenheimer

Fodor's Travel Publications
New York • Toronto • London • Sydney • Auckland

www.fodors.com

CREDITS
Writer: Lisa Oppenheimer

Series Editor: Karen Cure
Editor: Andrea Lehman
Editorial Production: Brian Vitunic
Production/Manufacturing: Robert B. Shields

Design: Fabrizio La Rocca, *creative director*;
Tigist Getachew, *art director*
Illustration and Series Design: Rico Lins, Keren Ora
Admoni/Rico Lins Studio

ABOUT THE WRITER

Lisa Oppenheimer, mother of two, is a contributor to
Disney, Sesame Street Parents, Family Life and *Car & Travel*
and the author of *Fodor's Around Los Angeles with Kids.*

Fodor's Around Boston with Kids

Copyright © 2001 by Fodor's Travel Publications

First Edition
ISBN 0–679–00460–2
ISSN 1531–3349

Important Tip

Although all prices, opening times, and other details in this
book are based on information supplied to us at press time,
changes occur all the time in the travel world, and Fodor's
cannot accept responsibility for facts that become outdated
or for inadvertent errors or omissions. So always confirm
information when it matters, especially if you're making a
detour to visit a specific place.

Special Sales

Fodor's Travel Publications are available at special discounts
for bulk purchases for sales promotions or premiums. Special
editions, including personalized covers, excerpts of existing
guides, and corporate imprints, can be created in large
quantities for special needs. For more information, contact
your local bookseller or Special Markets, Fodor's Travel
Publications, 280 Park Avenue, 10th floor, New York, NY
10017. Inquiries from Canada should be directed to your
local Canadian bookseller or sent to Random House of
Canada, Ltd., Marketing Dept., 2775 Matheson Boulevard
East, Mississauga, Ontario L4W 4P7. Inquiries from the
United Kingdom should be sent to Fodor's Travel
Publications, 20 Vauxhall Bridge Road, London, England
SW1V 2SA.

CONTENTS

WELCOME TO GREAT DAYS!

Everyone knows that organizing a family's schedule is a full-time job. Pickups, drop-offs, school, parties, after-school activities—everyone off in their own direction. Of course, it's an organizer's dream, but a scheduling nightmare. Spending time together shouldn't be another thing to have to figure out.

We know what's it's like to try to find good places to take your children or grandchildren. Sometimes it's tough to change plans when you suddenly hear about a kid-friendly event; besides, a lot of those events end up being crowded or, worse, sold out. It's also hard to remember places you read about in a newspaper or magazine, and sometimes just as hard to tell from the description what age group they're geared to. There's nothing like bringing a "grown-up" 12-year-old to an activity that's intended for his 6-year-old sister. Of course, if you're visiting Boston, it's even harder to figure out the best things to do with your kids before you even get there. That's where we come in.

What you'll find in this book are 68 ways to have a terrific couple of hours or an entire day with your children or your grandchildren. We've scoured the city, digging out activities your kids will love—from the historic buildings of the Freedom Trail to the newfangled technology of the Museum of Science. The best part is that it's stress-free, uncomplicated, and easy for you. Open the book to any page and find a helpful description of a kid-friendly attraction, with age ratings to make sure it's right for your family, smart tips on visiting so that you can get the most out of your time there, and family-friendly eats nearby. The address, telephone number, open hours, and admission prices are all there for your convenience. We've done the work, so you don't have to.

Those with special interests, or anyone who loves tours, should check out airports, newspapers, universities, and large corporations, many of which offer tours. Newcomers to Boston can get their bearings at Unforgettable Boston, a new interactive movie playing near the New England Aquarium.

WAYS TO SAVE MONEY
We list only regular adult, student (with I.D.), and kids' prices; children under the ages specified are free. It always pays to

ask at the ticket booth whether any discounts are offered for a particular status or affiliation (but don't forget to bring your I.D.). Discounts are often available for senior citizens, AAA members, military personnel, and veterans, among others. Many attractions offer family memberships, generally good for one year of unlimited use for your family. These memberships sometimes allow you to bring a guest. Prices vary, but the memberships often pay for themselves if you visit the attraction several times a year. Sometimes there are other perks: newsletters or magazines, members-only previews, and discounts at a gift shop, for parking, or for birthday parties or special events. If you like a place when you visit, you can sometimes apply the value of your one-day admission to a membership if you do it before you leave.

Look for coupons—which can often save you $2–$3 per person—everywhere from the local newspaper to a supermarket display to your pediatrician's office. In addition, sometimes groups of attractions get together and offer combination tickets, which are cheaper than paying for each one individually. One such bargain is City Pass, which covers admission to six local attractions—the Isabella Stuart Gardner Museum, John F. Kennedy Library and Museum, John Hancock Observatory, Museum of Fine Arts, Museum of Science, and New England Aquarium—for about half the cost of separate entry. City Pass is available at each attraction as well as through many hotels.

Also keep an eye out for attractions—mostly museums and other cultural destinations—that offer free admission one day a month or one day a week after a certain time. We've noted several in this book.

WHEN TO GO

With the exception of seasonal attractions, kid-oriented destinations are generally busiest when children are out of school—especially weekends, holidays, and summer—but not necessarily. Attractions that draw school trips can be swamped with clusters of sometimes-inconsiderate children tall enough to block the view of your preschooler. But school groups tend to leave by early afternoon, so weekdays after 2 during the school year can be an excellent time to visit museums, zoos, and aquariums. For outdoor attractions, it's good to visit after a rain, since crowds will likely have cleared out.

The hours we list are the basic hours, not necessarily those applicable on holidays. Some attractions are closed when schools are closed, but others add extra hours on these days. It's always best to check if you want to see an attraction on a holiday.

SAFETY

Obviously the amount of vigilance necessary will depend on the attraction and the ages of your kids. In crowded attractions, keep an eye on your children at all times, as their ages warrant. When you arrive, point out what the staff or security people are wearing, and find a very visible landmark to use as a meeting place, should you get separated. If you do split into groups, pick a time to meet. This will decrease waiting time, help you and your kids get the most out of your time there, and manage everyone's expectations.

FINAL THOUGHTS

Actually, this time it's yours, not ours. We'd love to hear what you or your kids thought about the attractions you visited. Or if you happened upon a place that you think warrants inclusion, by all means, send it along, so the next family can enjoy Boston even more. You can e-mail us at editors@ fodors.com (specify the name of the book on the subject line), or write to us at Fodor's Around Boston with Kids, 280 Park Avenue, New York, NY 10017. We'll put your ideas to good use. In the meantime, have fun!

THE EDITORS!

AUTHOR'S PICKS:

Top Five:
Museum of Science
Children's Museum of Boston
New England Aquarium
George's Island
Boston Harbor Cruises Whale Watching

Best...
Outdoors: Purgatory Chasm
Wacky: Davis Mega-Maze
Cultural Activity: Museum of Fine Arts
New & Noteworthy: Six Flags New England
Museum: Museum of Science

ARCHERY USA

Given the dearth of archers with sneaker endorsements, it's no surprise that most kids know little about this ages-old sport. But once they get going, children are drawn in by the challenge of trying to hit that little gold circle with a tiny arrowhead, especially since the hand-eye coordination required rivals that of most video games.

Visitors to the indoor facility are first sized up to determine their shooting arm. First-time William Tells might be surprised to find that they're instructed to pull the string with their non-favored arm. Actually, your shooting stance is determined not by your dominant hand but by your dominant eye, which is easily tested on the spot. Everyone is then equipped with beginner bows (included in the cost) and sent on to the range.

Standing behind the green line, you fire at a target 20 yards away. Several targets are adjustable, so young children (or their parents!) can have it moved close enough for some arrows to find their mark. Once on deck, pay close attention to the four commands shouted (LOUDLY!) during the session: "On-line" (get into position), "Begin" (load bow

HEY, KIDS! When you think of precision engineering, you probably don't think of the good ol' bow and arrow. So you might be surprised that top Olympic archers routinely buy high-tech bows that cost thousands of dollars. Made of carbon compounds, these bows are engineered to withstand the pounding and vibrations that pros subject them to. Carbon arrows—designed for maximum aerodynamics (to fly faster and straighter)—are also extremely expensive. Needless to say, you're going to have to practice on the Chevy bow for a while before you can graduate to the Mercedes-Benz.

606 Providence Hwy.
(Rte. 1 northbound), Dedham

781/320-3606

 $10 per hr ages 17
and up, $8 per hr
children 16 and under

 T–Th 1–9, F 1–7, Sa–Su 1–6

 7 and up

and shoot), "Hold" (bring the string back to original position), and "Let Down" (an emergency command to stop what you're doing). This protocol is in place to ensure that no one fires while anyone is retrieving arrows (and vice versa).

According to owner Anthony Bellettini, children make up a large portion of archers here—about 6,000–8,000 kids a year. Part of the draw is the nature of competition: The goal is to achieve a personal best rather than to trounce your rival. The ultimate achievement, called a Robin Hood, entails shooting an arrow directly into the back of another arrow already in the target's center. (Don't get your hopes up!)

For obvious reasons, Archery USA runs a tight (and strict) ship—no horsing around and no running. No one, after all, wants to come off the range looking like Steve Martin in one of his old comedy routines.

KID-FRIENDLY EATS: T.G.I. Friday's (750 Providence Hwy., tel. 781/251–0650), next door, offers plentiful, tasty chain fare, plus crayons. For more homespun atmosphere, try the family-owned **Midway Restaurant** (269 Washington St., tel. 781/329–5575), whose vast menu includes seafood and salads as well as children's favorites.

KEEP IN MIND: With 20 lanes, Archery USA usually has some open, but big groups should reserve ahead. Staff here is certified, trained, licensed, and insured by the National Archery Association, the organization that runs the sport nationwide and selects teams for national and Olympic competition. To really improve, sign up for the 1½-hour classes (all ages). Classes (roughly $13 each) are offered Friday 7–8:30 and Saturday 9–10:30 and 11–12:30. Though students typically register for six weeks, drop-ins (to try it out) are often accommodated. Children 16 and under must be accompanied by a parent at all times.

ARNOLD ARBORETUM

I f the words "Botanical Garden" make you think "stuffy," think again. How stuffy can it really be if you can career around it on a pair of Rollerblades?

An unusual partnership between the folks at Harvard University and the Boston Parks and Recreation Department, this arboretum (founded in 1872) combines science with recreation, allowing visitors to appreciate the workings of the botanical world as well as its inherent pleasures. At 225 acres, the vast sweep of greenery is an unlikely surprise, particularly since it's tucked inside citified Jamaica Plain and its apartment houses and office buildings.

More than 13,000 labeled trees, shrubs, and other plants cover the acreage here, with something in bloom nearly all the time from February through late November. December and January are pretty blooming quiet, but then, who wants to walk in the winter cold anyway? Notable inhabitants include the Seven-Son Flower, an Asian plant that exists in only a few places in this country. The bonsai are usually a big hit with kids (look for them from mid-April to mid-November); some of these tiny little trees date back

HEY, KIDS!

Like animals, plant seeds have survival strategies. Maple seeds have "wings" to carry them away from the mother tree's shade. Willow trees produce seeds early in spring, when it's wet enough for them to sprout. As for fruit seeds, let's just say they're, er, distributed via animals' digestive systems.

KID-FRIENDLY EATS: The arboretum is within walking distance of all of the restaurants of downtown Jamaica Plain. One good choice is the **Centre Street Cafe** (669 Centre St., tel. 617/524–9217), where a world of foods from Tex-Mex to Asian features mostly organic ingredients. Dishes can be prepared to meet vegetarian needs. You'll need either a car or bike to get to **Doyle's** (3484 Washington St., tel. 617/524–2345), but the longtime neighborhood haunt's combination of pub fare and entrées is worth the trip.

125 Arborway (off Jamaica Way)

 617/524-1718

 Donations accepted

 Daily sunrise–sunset; Hunnewell
Building M–F 9–4, Sa–Su 12–4

All ages

to the mid-18th century. Indoor educational exhibits at the Hunnewell Building (including a few that are interactive) are worth a visit.

The genus and species of Arnold's plant life probably won't bowl younger children over. "Look, Mommy, pretty flowers!" is about the best you can hope for. Still, bright colors and wide-open spaces are definite attention grabbers, but don't forget to look where you're going if you're taking in the sights on a set of wheels (i.e., skates or bikes). Paved paths run for roughly 1½ miles around the grounds and are generally car-free (vehicles require a special permit). That, paired with the mostly flat terrain, makes this place so safe, it's become a haven for first-time bladers. There are a couple of hills, most notably Peter's Hill, from which you can get some great views of the Boston skyline.

KEEP IN MIND: Since trees are part of the scientific collection, tree climbing and ball playing (both of which might damage these centuries-old marvels) are strictly prohibited. Picnicking is also a no-no. The arboretum's biggest event is Lilac Sunday, held in mid-May. People have been coming since the turn of the 20th century to see the 500 lilacs (about 200 different kinds) in bloom. It's also the only day of the year when you're allowed to picnic. In addition, the event features entertainment and food vendors.

F ace it. Not all of us can be a genius with a glue gun or rival our children's school art teachers in ability and inspiration. Thankfully, there are some talented folks willing to share their knack for artistry at ArtBeat, an art supply store that offers open studio hours every afternoon. Here you and your little ones can dabble in spur-of-the-moment creative exploits together and—the best part for kids—play with some messy mixtures you might not let them touch at home.

Projects take from about 45 minutes to an hour. Look for decoupage (a type of glazed collage), doll making, candle making, picture frames, and more. Sometimes you'll get to choose from a list. At other times (mainly during school vacations, when the studio tends to get busy), you'll be guided by a theme.

Younger artists (starting at age 4) might appreciate some adult input, but staffers caution parents not to help too much. (The studio can't accommodate children under 4, but staff members will help you assemble materials to coach little ones in the featured craft at

KID-FRIENDLY EATS: If you're up for a tasty gastronomic adventure, try the Lebanese specialties of **Cafe Barada** (201 Massachusetts Ave., tel. 781/646–9650). The yogurt-cucumber salad is a big hit, and kids have been known to like the kebabs. Go to the Italian/Mediterranean **Neillio's** (218 Massachusetts Ave., tel. 781/643–6644) for absolutely wonderful fresh pastas—fettuccine, ravioli, and many others—with sauces to match.

212A Massachusetts Ave.,
East Arlington

 781/646-2200

 $5–$15

Studio hrs M–F 12–5, Sa–Su 3–5

4 and up

home.) Older children, on the other hand, might prefer to work independently. If that's the case, consider pulling up a chair and doing a project of your own.

For those who fear an art workshop more than the auto repair shop, fear not. There's no pressure to produce a Picasso. Owner Jan Whitted stresses that ability is secondary to desire. "You're free to be a beginner," she says. The ArtBeat atmosphere is homey, and instructors are pleasant. Their aim is just to spark your family's imagination enough so you enjoy the experience and perhaps continue flexing your creative muscles on your own.

KEEP IN MIND:
Though the store itself is open much of each day, studio hours are limited, and you must arrive at least an hour before the studio's closing to take part in a craft. Occasionally, a few slots open up before 3 on weekends, so if you're feeling the urge to create then, give a call. In fact, it's a good idea to call ahead for reservations at all times, since the studio is small.

HEY, KIDS! Challenge yourself by trying something completely different. Even if the activity of the day is painting, you don't have to stick to the same old routine. Staff members will be happy to show you some different painting techniques, such as sponging, dry brushing, or stenciling.

BATTLESHIP COVE

E very war produces military legends, but few are bigger—in the purely literal sense— than World War II's "Big Mamie." Mamie, as it happens, is not a "who" but a "what"— the enormous Battleship *Massachusetts,* nicknamed Mamie by her crew. The vessel currently resides at Battleship Cove, part of a stationary fleet assembled as a memorial to Massachusetts residents who died in combat.

For kids, this is pay dirt in the naval history and adventuring department. Several floating monuments—in addition to Mamie, the military craft here include the U.S.S. *Joseph P. Kennedy, Jr.,* a destroyer; two PT boats; and a submarine—are open for exploration. (There's also a Vietnam War–era helicopter and a Japanese suicide boat, but you'll have to appreciate those from the outside only.) Wander through the Mamie from top to nearly bottom, examining the engine room, poking around crew quarters, and even positioning the artillery (you can aim some of the battleship's 40-mm guns, but you can't fire them). The 690-foot ship seems large until you realize she accommodated more than 2,000 sailors at a time.

HEY, KIDS!

Just how big is the *Massachusetts?* This sturdy lady is as long as two football fields, and, if she were on land, would stand taller than four two-story homes stacked on top of one another. How much does she weigh? Oh, a mere 46,000 tons.

KEEP IN MIND: While you're down this way, visit the *Bounty* (10 N. Main St., tel. 508/673–3886), a tall ship replica built for the 1962 film *Mutiny on the Bounty;* it's available for touring when it's in port. During summers at Heritage State Park (200 Davol St., tel. 508/675–5759), able sailors can use sailboats for a nominal charge. Other local sights include the Marine Museum (70 Water St., tel. 508/674–3533), an antique carousel at Battleship Cove (tel. 508/324–4300), and the Old Colony & Fall River Railroad Museum (tel. 508/674–9340).

Rte. 24 Exit 7, Fall River

 Early Apr–June and early Sept–late Oct, daily 9–5; July–early Sept, daily 9–6; late Oct–early Apr, daily 9–4:30

508/678–1100 or 800/533–3194

 $9 ages 15 and up, $4.50 children 6–14

 All ages

That's nothing next to the cramped quarters of the submarine *Lionfish*. Roam the confines of this 311-foot underwater tube, and imagine sharing it with 81 grown men. It'll remind you that none of these ladies was built to be glamorous, but neither are they personality-less hulls. They have enormous sentimental value, particularly to those who manned them a half century ago. On many days you'll find devoted former crew members aboard the Mamie just to give her a fresh spit shine.

Though most visitors are day-trippers, the Mamie hosts a large number of overnighters as well. Most are school and scout groups, but families can join in if there's room—just give a call. You'll get to sleep in the same battleship quarters the crew slept in (assuming you consider this a good thing!), but you'll enjoy a much better "mess" of chicken, mashed potatoes, and gravy (breakfast and lunch are included, too).

KID-FRIENDLY EATS: You can get on-board chow (hot dogs, hamburgers, clam chowder, and the like) at the **snack bar.** (You can also bring your own food as long as you eat it in the snack bar area.) If you want to eat off the ship, try **Applebee's Neighborhood Grill** (311 Plymouth Ave., tel. 508/675–1110), where the grub includes salads, sandwiches, soups, and a kids' menu.

BLUE HILLS TRAILSIDE MUSEUM
AND RESERVATION

For such a cosmopolitan city, Boston is surrounded by a surprising amount of open space. Case in point: the Blue Hills Reservation. This giant slice of the great outdoors is positively Eden-like. You'll never believe you're only 10 miles from the city.

At 7,000 acres, the reservation is a vast hunk of nature. More than 150 miles of trails crisscross the place, accommodating explorers on mountain bikes or on foot. (In-line skaters are out of luck as there are no paved paths.) The highest elevations provide some striking views.

But all that's just the beginning. Winter warriors can speed downhill on the slopes at Blue Hills Ski Area (4001 Washington St., Canton, tel. 781/828–7490) or enjoy the reservation's trails cross-country style. Warm-weather wanderers can refresh themselves with a dip in Houghton's Pond. Year-round you can get in the saddle and mosey the trails on horseback (see below).

KID-FRIENDLY EATS: Your closest choice is **Doodad's Dine & Deli** (2790 Washington St., Canton, tel. 781/828–4010) for sandwiches and other casual eats. Don't let the Canton address fool you; the restaurant is only steps away, a big bonus if you're starving after an active day outside. On the edge of the reservation, you can get home cookin' at **Newcomb Farms** (1139 Randolph Ave., tel. 617/698–95447). The cozy place serves those all-important brunch dishes as well as tasty sandwiches, grills, salads, and just about anything else you can think of.

Nature lovers can learn a little more about the area at the on-site Blue Hills Trailside Museum. Appropriately named (it is indeed located next to the trails), the small facility is, in effect, a scaled-down version of the reservation, representing the park's different habitats, including woodland, pond, and wetland. A few nifty indoor features include a natural honey factory (AKA a beehive—windows let you watch the action) and a full-size Wetu, a bark structure once used by Massachusetts Indians. The museum's outdoor acreage—16 acres in all—includes a self-guided pond walk and a number of animal enclosures. For an optimal afternoon, start your adventure at the museum, where you can park and purchase the all-important map. Spend the rest of the day wending your way around the trails. Those who skip the inside exhibits don't have to miss out on the museum completely. Animal habitats for white-tailed deer, river otters, red-tailed hawks, and other animals are open even when the museum isn't and can be viewed free of charge.

HEY, KIDS! Wonder why there are stone walls in the Blue Hills woods? They were property boundaries, built by 18th-century farmers. Blue Hills is actually what's called a second-growth forest. Most of the original trees were cleared for farming in the late 1700s. Miraculously, the forest has rejuvenated itself, thanks to nature's reseeding.

KEEP IN MIND: Make sure to ask about the museum's numerous programs, including Maple Sugar Days (March) and school-vacation events. As for horseback riding, the St. Moritz stable (629 Willard St., tel. 617/472–0649) offers trail rides for those aged 12 and up on weekdays 9–5 and weekends 12–5. The Paddocks (1010 Hillside St., tel. 617/698–1884), which accommodates children as young as 10, operates Tuesday through Sunday 9–5. Both stables operate year-round, charge $30 an hour, and require reservations. Please note: Trails are for walking; no trotting, etc., is allowed.

BOSTON BY SEA

Boston has made a cottage industry out of historic walking tours. Unfortunately, some of the city's most history-rich territory—that lying offshore in the Boston Harbor—is a bit hard to stroll around on your own. Luckily, the folks at the Boston History Collaborative have created the next best thing: a lively 90-minute presentation that details hundreds of years of Boston maritime facts. Staged on a three-level harbor cruiser, the show uses live performers, video, and the scenery outside your window to chronicle the harbor's role in history.

Two actors with a trunk full of props run the show. In addition to spinning yarns and singing songs, the pair channel a cast of bygone characters (a nautical "powder monkey" and a pirate, among them) seemingly with the change of a hat. Guests—particularly young ones—can quite literally be swept into the action as these tireless thespians concoct their stories. It's an engaging way to learn a thing or two. The concept—to paint a

HEY, KIDS!
Want to be a pirate? Late in the show, young visitors are recruited to unfurl the Jolly Roger (the black skull and crossbones flag that commonly flew on pirate ships) and cavort around the decks with Calico Jack. Your reward for your efforts is a bit of pirate booty: candy.

KEEP IN MIND: Tours leave from the end of Long Wharf rain or shine, and indoor seating (there's outdoor seating, too) makes this a nifty rainy-day activity. Most of the performance takes place inside on the boat's second level, but the narration is audible throughout. Seats on the port side give you the best look at sights as they are being described by the actors. As always, dress for your destination. Temperature on the water can be a lot cooler than on land, so bring your trusty sweater.

picture of what the harbor used to look like—is a little like the landlocked Old Town Trolley tours (*see below*), except that you can't (or shouldn't) get on and off along the way. Even that may change in the future, as organizers ponder ways to team up with some attractions.

Tours include lots of information—too much for anyone to absorb all at once—but the content has been designed to allow you to walk in and out without feeling that you've fallen behind. Details range from the significance of the "Golden Stairs" (where many New England–bound immigrants first set foot on American soil) to the harbor's previous designation as a "toilet" (the once filthy water is much cleaner these days thanks to concerted effort). Other sights along the way include George's Island, Boston Light, Castle Island, and the U.S.S. *Constitution* (see listings for each). An extra perk for budding aviators: You'll pass close enough to the airport to want to duck when those jumbo jets make their approaches.

KID-FRIENDLY EATS: Soft drinks and snacks are served at the on-board **snack bar.** If you're happy by the water, grab a picnic and enjoy the view at the end of Long Wharf. If you've got a craving for Italian, try Fanueil Hall's **Il Panino** (120 Fanueil Hall, tel. 617/573–9700), where you can make yourself happy with some great salads, pastas, and risottos and make the kids happy with tasty pizzas. And of course, the vast number of other Quincy Market eateries are also at your disposal (see Fanueil Hall, below).

BOSTON COMMON

The first thing you need to know about this public park is that it's called the "Common" (singular), as opposed to the "Commons" (plural). The savannah of Boston's urban jungle for more than three centuries, the Common started out in the 1600s as a communal grazing ground for local farm cows (hence the name). The pastoral image was sorely tainted by the advent of public hangings and floggings, not to mention the encampment of British soldiers during the Revolutionary War. Thankfully, today's pastimes are more sanguine.

Despite various efforts to divide and sell it (and the no-doubt salacious glances from private developers), the Common has endured as public property. Today it maintains its status as the city's gathering ground, as evidenced by such noteworthy 20th-century events as a speech by Martin Luther King, Jr., and a visit by the Pope.

Still, causes are not required to congregate. On these 48 acres in the middle of the city, there's plenty of room to simply throw a ball or push a stroller, all the while soaking up fresh air. Climbing, sliding, and playing in the sand are the inherent joys of the good-size

KID-FRIENDLY EATS: Up in the theater district, **Bennigan's** (191 Stuart St., tel. 617/227–3754) boasts the large chain menu we all know and love, plus tools for coloring. Also see an option under Swan Boats at the Public Garden.

Visitor center, 145 Tremont St.

Boston Common 888/733–2678,
617/635–7383 Boston Park Rangers

 Free

Daily sunrise–11 PM

All ages

playground. Shallow Frog Pond—neither a real pond nor a home for frogs—lures thousands of kids to cool off in its fountain each summer. In winter, when Frog freezes over, the place becomes to Boston what the Rockefeller Center ice rink is to New York.

History buffs can scope out the park's historical significance by perusing some of the landmarks. Monuments include the Boston Massacre Memorial, created in 1888 by Robert Kraus, and the Shaw Memorial, an 1897 structure honoring the Union Army's first free black regiment. The centuries-old Central Burying Ground is also located here.

HEY, KIDS! Check out this 17th-century English in a city proclamation: "Noe comon marish and Pastur Ground shall herafter bye gifte or sayle, exchange, or otherwise, be counted unto property without consent of ye major part of ye inhabitants of ye towne." In 21st-century terms, it forbade the sale of any of the Common's grounds.

KEEP IN MIND: Frog Pond Ice Skating (tel. 617/635–2120) usually starts the first week in November and goes through early to mid-March, daily 10–10. Concerts and special events are often held on the Common. Call the Boston Parks and Recreation Department (tel. 617/635–4505) for information about them as well as about the annual summer Shakespeare on the Common.

BOSTON DUCK TOURS

One if by land, two if by sea, three if by...Duck. OK, it's not exactly Longfellow, but Boston Duck Tours actually take you by land *and* by sea (or at least the Charles River). Don't confuse these tours with the Make Way for Ducklings Tour (*see below*). These "Ducks" are an actual mode of transportation, namely authentic WWII amphibious vehicles currently used as tour buses. The fleet of 17 steel waders spirit visitors around Boston, first on terra firma and eventually heading down the ramp near the Museum of Science to end up afloat (by design, of course) in the Charles. If the idea of touring historic Boston doesn't excite your kids, these quirky contraptions, which look like a cross between a military truck and a jungle boat, almost certainly will.

Tours last roughly 80–90 minutes. Along the way, Ducks waddle by important Boston sights and neighborhoods, including Beacon Hill, downtown Boston, and several sights on the Freedom Trail. Splashdown comes about a third of the way through. Once on water, children may even be invited to take the wheel (provided the water is calm). Narration is provided by lively "Con-DUCK-tors," who add a farcical flair to the adventure; on any given

HEY, KIDS!

The term "Duck" actually evolved from the WWII army abbreviation DUKW. "D" stood for the design year (1942); "U" for utility vehicle, "K" for front-wheel drive, and "W" for double rear axle (go figure these!). Is it any wonder that soldiers just called them Ducks?

KEEP IN MIND: Ducks are open-air vehicles, covered only by a canopy. Plastic side shields are lowered in cool or rainy weather, but you'll still be exposed to the elements, so dress appropriately. At press time, individual tickets were sold in person only (group sales available by phone) at the Center Court, inside the Prudential Center. You can purchase them up to two days ahead, a good idea in summer, when tours are often sold out by noon. Vehicles depart from outside the building, though that may change in the future.

day, your driver could be the fearless Captain Courageous or the caped Captain Ridiculous. Outrageous getups aside, these captains are serious navigators with extensive knowledge of Boston history, and they have sea and land licenses that enable them to maneuver Boston both by river and road (the latter qualifying as a military operation all by itself).

Unlike some other tours, the Duck trips are not stop-and-go excursions, meaning you won't be able to get out and amble around the various sights. Duck operators consider tours an overview of the city, and they encourage you to walk around it afterward. You might, then, consider the expedition the perfect Boston intro-DUCK-tion.

KID-FRIENDLY EATS: Despite its name, **Back Bay Brewing Co.** (755 Boylston St., tel. 617/424–8300) welcomes children with spaghetti and grilled cheese. Adults can opt for pasta, sandwiches, salads, and, of course, some home-grown brews. There's plenty of Italian food at **Vinny Testa's** (867 Boylston St., tel. 617/262–6699), and there are dozens of restaurants right in the Prudential Center (see below).

BOSTON HARBOR CRUISES WHALE WATCHING

Northeasterners can be forgiven their skepticism about actually seeing whales on a whale watch. Most of us, after all, are unaccustomed to seeing any wild animal more exotic than a garbage-can-variety raccoon, much less Moby Dick tooling around free in our own backyard. But hop a three-hour jaunt on Boston Harbor Cruises for a whale-watching excursion, and, amazingly, that's exactly what you'll find: great, blubberish creatures lumbering around the waters of Massachusetts. It's sure to make nature lovers of even the most reticent outdoor adventurer.

High-speed catamarans zoom out to Stelwagon Bank, where dozens of school-bus-size creatures await. Look for humpback, finback, and the diminutive (at least in whale terms) minke whales as well as the occasional dolphin. For the record, Moby Dick doesn't actually live here; he was a sperm whale, most of whom live in deeper waters. Awe-inspiring happenings during the roughly hour-long "show" include spouting and trumpeting (the deep-throated sound that accompanies spouting). Keep your eyes peeled for signs of other activities. The liftoff of birds (many of whom dog the whales for their "leftovers") could

KEEP IN MIND: Though you'll be at sea for roughly three hours, two of those hours will be spent getting to and from the sighting area, so bring activities and snacks. Dress warmly no matter what time of year you're traveling, as the sea air brings a chill. Use your camera sparingly; you'll miss a lot if you limit your gaze to the narrow confines of a viewfinder. Among the numerous other whale-watching expeditions in the area are A.C. Cruise Line (290 Northern Ave., tel. 800/422–8419) and one through the New England Aquarium (Central Wharf, tel. 617/973–5206).

63 Long Wharf

617/227-4321

$28 ages 13 and up,
$22 children 4–12

 Departures mid-May–mid-Sept, M–F 10:30 and
12:30, Sa–Su 8:30, 10:30, 12:30, 2:30, and 5:30

5 and up

mean a whale is coming to the surface, and a fast dive might be the precursor to a breach, that coveted, albeit only occasional, dramatic leap in the air.

Perhaps most amazing is proximity. Just how close will you get? Probably close enough to smell the whale's—ahem—aromatic breath. (The smell comes from bacteria in the whale spout.)

Whale-watching trips are suspended in late fall and winter, when the whales return to their warm Caribbean homes. But never fear: The plentiful supply of sand eels brings them back north each spring. Sightings are guaranteed; in the unlikely event of a no-show, the cruise line will give you a ticket good for passage any time (no cash refunds, however).

HEY, KIDS! Did you know that whales eat the equivalent of 8,000 quarter-pounders a day just to keep their whale-ish figures? And though they all may look alike to you, humpback whales have very distinctive markings on the underside of the tails. Can you tell them apart?

KID-FRIENDLY EATS: Steps away from the dock, **Tia's** (200 Atlantic Ave., tel. 617/227–0828) specializes in all kinds of seafood—but no whale. Moms and dads can enjoy lobster or swordfish while kids get their own favorites: grilled cheese, chicken nuggets, and burgers. A few more steps down the street, **Joe's American Bar & Grill** (100 Atlantic Ave., tel. 617/367–8700) features an enormous menu of sandwiches, grills, and entrées.

BOSTON LIGHT

Anyone who thinks the Maytag repairman is the loneliest person on earth ought to talk to the guys on Little Brewster Island. These hearty souls staff the island's famous lighthouse—Coast Guard Light Station Boston, nicknamed Boston Light—the oldest lighthouse site in North America. The 220-year-old edifice is plopped 10 miles from downtown Boston, center stage in a small mound of rock and grass merely 600 feet long and 250 feet wide. Suffice it to say that a winter tour of duty here is a particularly long and lonely time.

But Little Brewster residents are feeling a bit less forlorn these days, now that they're entertaining guests. Back in 1999, the U.S. Coast Guard teamed up with the Island Alliance and the National Park Service to open up the diminutive island for public tours. Oh sure, visitors could drop by before, but until recently, when public transportation was launched, getting here took either a private boat or a mighty strong pair of arms.

HEY, KIDS!
Look for the names of keepers carved into the island's rocks. No one's sure exactly how many there are. Suffice it to say, you'll find dozens dating all the way back to George Worthylake, Boston Light's original keeper. Worthylake drowned off the island in 1718.

KEEP IN MIND: Purchase tickets by phone or at the Harbor Islands Store, U.S. Courthouse Arcade (1 Courthouse Way, Fan Pier). Reservations are highly recommended (past summers have sold out). Attached to the courthouse is a small interactive discovery center dedicated to the Boston Harbor Islands. If you've got your own boat, you're welcome to visit the island Friday–Sunday (donation requested). Children under 50" are not permitted to climb the tower, but many enjoy the island anyway.

Island Alliance, 408 Atlantic Ave.

 $25 ages 13 and up,
$15 children 6–12

 Mid-May–mid-Oct, F–Su 10 and 2

617/223–8666

 6 and up

There's little fanfare on this acre of land with six structures, but the lighthouse makes it worth the trip. Like much of Boston, the little building is steeped in history, from its construction in 1716 to its reconstruction after the British blew it to pieces in 1776.

You'll travel to the island on the 49-passenger *Hurricane*. Once there, you'll be invited to haul yourself up the lighthouse's 76 stairs, followed by two ladders, an unappealing prospect to some. The rewards are some stellar views of the harbor and surrounding islands. The island also has a small exhibit dedicated to the structure.

Boston Light's official role is for navigation and weather reporting, but the real function seems to be symbolic. Most of today's lighthouses are automated and have long been abandoned by official staff. In fact, Boston Light is the country's only beacon operated by active Coast Guard personnel, who keep watch over a wide swath of ocean and a little slice of history.

KID-FRIENDLY EATS: Walk toward Fanueil Hall and you'll find the **Green Dragon Tavern** (11 Marshall St., tel. 617/367–0055), a Colonial tavern with huge pub portions to fill you up after your outdoor adventure. Half-portions of Italian favorites at **L'Osteria Restaurant** (104 Salem St., tel. 617/723–7847), in the North End, will probably be plenty for kids. (If you're going for lunch, call ahead to make sure they're open.)

BOSTON TEA PARLOUR

Once upon a time, tea was the focal point of an afternoon. Each day at 4, ladies (and perhaps gentlemen) would drop what they were doing and settle down in the formal parlor for a sip of chamomile. Alas, the tradition has been watered down. Most people are too busy to spread the formal tablecloth at teatime, and it's hard to feel ladylike when you're slurping from a Styrofoam cup bought on the fly at the Dunkin' Donuts drive through.

Boston Tea Parlour owner Cynthia Alex has done her best to re-create those genteel days, however. She has dressed up her pretty little Victorian tea cottage in lace, crystal, and tapestry, even adorning her servers in traditional black and white. Dainty music plays while mothers, grandmothers, and daughters (we're not trying to be sexist here; it's just that the overwhelming sentiment is that tea is just not a "guy" thing) sip tea and nibble away at elegant Victorian tables surrounded by scads of pretty trinkets.

Light fare includes salads, scones, and sandwiches. Pint-size sippers will be delighted by the "Little Princess" fare (for children 11 and under), which includes selections of heart-

HEY, KIDS! The tradition of tea supposedly began in Bedford, England—a significant fact since Ms. Alex's parlor is in Bedford, Massachusetts. The legend goes that an impatient (and hungry!) duchess ordered her servants to tote up a spread of sweets and beverages to quell her hunger until dinner. The idea was a hit and was subsequently adopted by all the ladies of status.

shape tea sandwiches (even peanut butter and fluff!) as well as fruit, dessert, and beverage. Decaffeinated cherry vanilla tea may appeal to the kids, but they can opt for fruit punch if they prefer.

Occasional events include visits by princesses, such as Cinderella, or perhaps even Mrs. Claus. The parlor hosts exceptional birthday parties (for children as young as 4), which include elegant private rooms, dress up, and crafts. Girls get to don a special boa during their stay, and all little guests get to take home a little bauble in the form of a piece of costume jewelry.

You don't have to get dressed up for the occasion—lots of moms and kids come in after school—but coming in chapeaus and lacy frocks definitely adds to the experience. Oh, and don't forget to lift your pinkies.

KEEP IN MIND:
Boston Tea Parlour isn't the only tea in town. Boston proper boasts two hallowed but pricier tea halls: the Ritz-Carlton (15 Arlington St., tel. 617/536–5700) and the Four Seasons (200 Boylston St., tel. 617/338–4400), which runs $22.50. Plan to get dolled up.

KID-FRIENDLY EATS: You'll probably get plenty to eat during your tea, but if you need more food, try out the delectable salads, breads, and sandwiches at the **Carriage House Cafe** (200 Great Rd., tel. 781/275–0095). If all the gourmet stuff is wearing on your little tea-loving teetotaler, you can always opt for **Friendly's** (343A Great Rd., tel. 781/275–0780), just down the road.

BOSTON TEA PARTY SHIP

One night 2¼ centuries ago, a group of colonists descended on Boston Harbor dressed as Native Americans. Steaming about the injustice of "taxation without representation," they dunked hundreds of crates of unfairly taxed tea into the drink. As any student steeped in American history (not to mention punning) can tell you, that event started the brew that eventually boiled over into the American Revolution.

The *Brig Beaver II,* a full-scale, working replica of the smallest of the three ships assailed that December night in 1773 (note the attraction's easy-to-remember phone number), re-creates the protest. As part of ongoing shows, costumed colonists host a rousing and often heated town meeting, during which you can join in with traditional cries of "Fie" at the mention of unfair taxation and toss out suggestions for defying British rule. The course of action is put to a vote, but throwing the tea in the harbor always wins out over such creative ideas as stealing it and drinking it. Then it's off to the *Beaver II* to conduct the deed. Kids and adults alike take part in dumping the precious cargo, in reality, empty crates tethered to the ship by ropes.

HEY, KIDS!

How much tea went over the edge? More than 300 crates. Talk about a major download! The tea was worth roughly $33,000 then—probably over $1 million today— enough to hit King George squarely in his wallet. No wonder the event burned the Brits so much and caused them to act!

KEEP IN MIND: Though many historic attractions are good for kids studying the period, this particularly lively show often appeals to little ones as well. The ship's official season ends during the icy months of December, January, and February, but the attraction occasionally opens on balmy December days. The ship also conducts a reenactment on the Sunday before December 16, the Tea Party's actual anniversary. (You'll have to watch from the bridge, as the throngs of spectators would probably sink the boat.) The precise site of the event is marked by a plaque on a nearby commercial building, at 470 Atlantic Avenue.

Afterward, rabble-rousers are invited to tour the rest of the ship. Look for information about the original *Beaver,* which was sunk by a hurricane at the end of the 18th century, and about construction of the replica. Budding sailors can try their hand at the time-honored skill of knot tying. There's also an exhibit dedicated to the significance of tea itself. Though it's lost out to coffee over the years, tea was a Colonial favorite that appealed to both genders, enabling women to take part in political chats formerly reserved for men's smoking rooms. Such an onerous levy on something considered a staple was simply more than locals could abide.

KID-FRIENDLY EATS: Just a few steps down the street, **Three Cheers** (290 Congress St., tel. 617/423–6166) has pub fare as well as a children's menu. About a five-minute walk to the other side of the Northern Avenue Bridge gets you to the **Barking Crab** (88 Sleeper St., tel. 617/426–2722), known for its reasonably priced fresh seafood. For kids, there are land-born entrées (such as burgers), too. The tasty crab-shack fare can be enjoyed inside or, in season, under the tent.

BOULDER MORTY'S

From the bottom, the edifices that make up Boulder Morty's don't seem so daunting. From the top—well, that's another story. Fortunately, you'll be so busy trying to figure out which hand or foot goes where (like a vertical game of Twister), you won't have time to notice how high you really are.

Though it seems every gym this side of Pike's Peak has spawned some sort of indoor rock climbing, Morty's (about 45 minutes from Boston) has given it a new dimension. Eight thousand square feet of climbing surfaces make the place a rarity in the northeast, a 40-station indoor mountain range spanning from a smooth novice climb to a jagged inverted peak.

Novice climbers first need to get the hang of belaying. The belayer holds the safety end of the rope and keeps the line taut enough to protect the climber from sudden drops. The $34 fee for the one-time introductory class, which includes equipment and climbing time, makes for a big initial investment, but once you've passed, you'll just pay for

HEY, KIDS!

Think you've mastered the art of indoor climbing? Think again. Morty's continually changes the configuration of climbing pegs to keep things interesting. For the greatest challenge, follow the black-and-orange-striped tags (tag colors indicate degree of difficulty).

KEEP IN MIND: Staff are always on hand for introductory classes. No reservations are necessary, but owner Ken Silber advises newcomers to call an hour or so ahead to avoid a wait. You can rent shoes for $6, but sneakers (preferably old ones—they might take a beating) are fine. A good rule for clothing: Keep it loose, but not too loose, lest you hear your children chanting from below, Al see London, I see France...£

a day pass and equipment. (Children under 12 don't need the class; they're not old enough to belay.)

Don't worry about getting your money's worth. Kids (and parents) often want to spend the day here—even in summer, since it's air-conditioned—and everyone goes home happily worn out. As for safety concerns, you'll have to sign the requisite waiver, but the protected environment, monitored by pros, feels very secure. The biggest risk seems to be to parents' egos, inevitably bruised when children grossly outperform their folks.

In between ascents, take five in the upstairs loft. The tables and chairs here make a perfect spot from which to marvel at some of the more experienced climbers. Crawling around the walls, they seem to defy gravity, like real-life Spidermen. ?It's like a ballet,£ says one—a ballet 35 feet off the ground.

KID-FRIENDLY EATS: Food from home can be stashed in the upstairs fridge while you climb, or you can order in from any number of restaurant menus that are kept at the front desk. If you'd rather eat out, you can find awesome deli sandwiches at the **Nashua Garden** (121 Main St., tel. 603/886–7363). The large menu (steaks, seafood, sandwiches, salads, kids' menu) at **Martha's Exchange** (185 Main St., tel. 603/883–8781) will please just about everyone, and there's even home-grown brews.

BUNKER HILL MONUMENT

Asking "Where was the Battle of Bunker Hill fought?" at first sounds like the equivalent of "What color was George Washington's white horse?" But the answer might surprise you. The infamous battle was actually fought on Breed's Hill (where the monument stands today), a slightly shorter mound of land about ½ mile south of the hill for which the battle is named. Why the discrepancy? It's anybody's guess. Some say the move was strategic (Breed's Hill is actually closer to Boston, making it an earlier point to head off the British); others chalk it up to plain old mis-navigation born of a bad map and a dark night.

Either way, the feisty, decidedly unconventional Colonial army effectively surprised the British, constructing a rudimentary fort and digging in for the good fight. (For the record, the proper Brits considered hiding behind barriers to be entirely unsportsmanlike.) At sunrise on June 17, 1775, the British, who had been camped nearby, awoke to find the fort in place. They attacked, and, after three assaults in two hours, walked away with a victory. But it was not without a sacrifice, as they lost half of their 2,200 soldiers.

KEEP IN MIND: A short walk away, a vivid telling of the battle can be found at the Charlestown Navy Yard Visitor Center (55 Constitution Rd., tel. 617/242–5601), formerly called the Bunker Hill Pavilion. Entitled "Whites of Their Eyes," (a phrase commonly—if erroneously—associated with Bunker Hill), the 18-minute presentation ($3 adults, $1.50 children 18 and under) operates April through December 9:30 to 4:30. Certain elements, such as the headless soldier, may be too ghoulish for some. June through August, ask about the schedule of musket-firing demonstrations. Children under 14 need to be accompanied up the stairs by an adult.

In season, National Park Service rangers give hourly talks (roughly 15 minutes each) on the historic encounter. Year-round, you'll find letters in which British and Colonial soldiers recount in detail the events that took place that night. "Nothing could be more shocking than the carnage that followed the storming of this work," reads one. Dioramas accurately re-create the scene just as the British and Colonials saw it. Even those not enamored of American history will be impressed by the perfection of these miniatures.

The 220-foot obelisk, completed in 1842, is a marvel in and of itself. Granite had to be hauled in from Quincy and then stacked by hand. And the views from the top of the monument's 294 stairs will make you realize why the vantage point was so valuable.

HEY, KIDS! Colonial-era muskets weren't very dependable. It took 15–20 seconds to re-load and shoot (a disadvantage when the enemy is advancing), and misfires were common, partly explaining why soldiers fired simultaneously. Besides, says one park ranger only half in jest, "If you only fire one, it's not very scary."

KID-FRIENDLY EATS: The **Warren Tavern** (2 Pleasant St., tel. 617/241–8142), a restoration of a 1780 Colonial tavern, has just about every kind of burger you can think of, even one named for Paul Revere (inexplicably with Swiss cheese and mushrooms). You can also choose from seafood, sandwiches, and salads. The **Ninety-Nine Restaurant** (29/31 Austin St., tel. 617/242–8999) has the chain's huge selection of hamburgers, salads, grills, and other entrées.

BUTTERFLY PLACE

Question: What has 1,000 wings and flies? Answer: The Butterfly Place (or at least its collective residents). Founded in 1990, this private, family-owned business was born out of a penchant for airborne entomology (owner George Leslie started raising moths when he was 6 years old). Today this unusual facility houses roughly 500 butterflies representing about 50 different species, all fluttering around a 3,100-square-foot walk-through atrium.

Visits here start with a 15-minute film on the facts of lepidopteran life (from caterpillar to butterfly), which will elicit "ewws" or "wows" depending on your child's disposition. Then it's off to the atrium. Budding horticulturalists will no doubt be impressed by the diverse plant life in the lovely indoor garden. The diversity represents what you might see in the tropics. Butterflies, like other notable beauties, are a pretty persnickety lot, each variety demanding its own set of perks. The monarch, for example, will only lay its eggs on the leaves of a milkweed plant.

HEY, KIDS!

To try to get a butterfly to land on you, stand very still. Wearing certain color clothes won't matter; the creatures can't tell them apart. Perfume is a bad idea, too; you won't fool them into thinking you're a flower. (Don't laugh; people have tried this!)

KID-FRIENDLY EATS:
Covered picnic benches provide a perfect spot to finish your nature expedition. For ribs, burgers, and chicken with an Aussie flare, try **Outback Steakhouse** (440 Middlesex Rd., tel. 978/649–8700). Aspiring firefighters may be distracted from eating by all the fire-fighting memorabilia at the **Firehouse Restaurant** (130 Middlesex Rd., tel. 978/649–4118). The huge menu includes burgers and steaks as well as homemade pot pies and pot roast.

Mr. Leslie breeds all the domestic varieties in-house; exotic inhabitants are recruited from spots like Florida and Costa Rica and hatched from pupae. (Lest you think about importing your own flock, think again; the pastime requires numerous permits.) Unhatched pupae are openly displayed, and if you're lucky, you might be able to watch a butterfly emerge. Or you might catch a praying mantis slowly preying on its dinner (a live wasp), a fascinating sight for those who can bear to look. At least one staff member is always on hand to answer questions and point out pertinent facts about the entomological world.

Do think carefully about how you dress for the occasion. Butterflies like their quarters warm—about 80°F. So even if it's cold outside, make sure to apparel in layers to keep comfortable.

KEEP IN MIND: The Butterfly Place welcomes all ages, but for the safety of these delicate creatures, children under 3 must be carried, kept in a stroller, or held by the hand. Visitors are free to gaze, gawk, and gander, but no grabbing. On the other hand, some precocious creatures might choose to temporarily perch on a fortunate visitor or two. Those who find such a prospect undelightful can simply give a gentle blow and they'll flutter off.

CASTLE ISLAND PARK

ontrary to what you might think from its name, a stroll to this popular park won't require a bathing suit, but you may want one while you're there. Castle Island isn't actually an island, though it was one when it was named (around the early 1600s). Since then, a causeway has joined this lovely crescent of land jutting out into the Boston Harbor—one of the farthest points you can venture to in the city without actually leaving dry land. That this faux island is today accessible on foot (as well as by car) makes it a haven for anyone out to enjoy the fresh air.

Roughly 2½ miles of promenade form a loop from Day Boulevard to Castle Island and back again. Pleasure Bay, the body of water at the center of the loop, is commonly referred to as Metropolitan Boston's largest swimming pool. You can access the water from any of the park's beaches. Paved paths around the bay accommodate different types of wheels—stroller, roller, or bike. A playground and fishing pier are perfect outdoor diversions. If you'd prefer to tarry, picnic tables and park benches are ideal spots from which to sip soft drinks and watch the scenery (the views of the Boston skyline are magnificent). After all that

KEEP IN MIND: Although Castle Island's park is open year-round, Ft. Independence can only be accessed (via tours) weekends from Memorial Day to Columbus Day. Tours are run by the Castle Island Association for the Metropolitan District Commission (tel. 617/727–5293). If you want to get spooked, take the Halloween Mystery Walk (call the MDC for info), an annual stroll through a ghoulishly decked-out fort. Castle Island is part of the larger Marine Park, which, in winter, includes the MDC's on-site skating rink.

drinking, you'll be happy know that this castle is modern-facility equipped; bathrooms, however, are only open April–October.

If you're wondering, the island got its name from its military significance. Numerous forts were built here over the centuries, all informally known as the "Castle." The most modern—Ft. Independence, which dominates the island—was built in the mid-19th century. You can wander outside the fort on your own, but you'll need a guided tour to get inside. In addition to its military legacy, the immense stone structure is purported to have been the site of buried treasure and sea-serpent sightings.

KID-FRIENDLY EATS: To truly appreciate the splendor here, you'll want to bring your own eats and enjoy them in the out-of-doors. In season, **Sullivan's,** an on-site institution in these parts, provides the perfect accessories for the expedition: hot dogs, snacks, and sodas. Another institution, this one a year-round restaurant, is the family-owned **Farragut House** (149 P St., tel. 617/268-1212), a friendly place for fish, steak, ribs, and children's specialties.

CHARLES RIVER CANOE AND KAYAK

Most people associate the Charles with the wide stretch that separates Boston from Cambridge. However, the river actually begins in Hopkinton and extends 80 miles—much of it through rural communities—before reaching Boston city limits. Quiet expanses between Hopkinton and Waltham, the point after which the river becomes broad, straighter, and urban, are enormously peaceful, winding through marshes and past turn-of-the-20th-century estates. Though it's only a half-hour drive from the city to the spot where you rent and launch your craft in Newton, you'll feel as if you're on the other side of the world.

Paddlers should keep a careful eye out for such resident wildlife as turtles—a big thrill for kids who've never seen one outside of a pet store tank. You'll have to look carefully, though, as the little green guys tend to blend in with the scenery. As for birds, you never know what you'll see, perhaps an enormous great blue heron, ospreys, or Eastern orioles. Even muskrats call the area home.

HEY, KIDS!

How many different kinds of turtles can you spot? The painted turtles are the little guys; the snapping turtles are the great big ones. Hint: Stay away from the big ones. They could bite. In fact, rangers say it's a good idea not to bother—or feed—any of the wildlife.

KEEP IN MIND:
Such marshy territory is prime critter country, so don't forget the bug spray. Flip-flops or water shoes are a good idea, too. Your feet will probably get a little wet as you climb in the boat, but the squishy, muddy ground might gross out little ones who go barefoot. If you'd prefer to city gaze as you paddle, try the company's satellite office in Allston Brighton (tel. 617/462–2513). Look for its kiosk at the dock across the Elliott Bridge from Harvard Square. For canoeing on a lake, try the company's office in Natick, on Lake Cochituate (tel. 508/647–1700).

2401 Commonwealth Ave.,
Newton

617/965-5110

Canoes $10 per hr; kayaks $11
per hr singles, $13 per hr dou-
bles, $5 per hour kids' kayaks

Apr–Oct, M–F 10–8, Sa–Su 9–8

All ages

Since rentals (which include the mandatory life jackets) are hourly, you'll also want to keep an eye on the time, for the sake of your bank account as well as your arms. Paddling one hour out, after all, means a second hour of paddling back, and that return trip can be a killer. You'll want to consider your direction, as heading downstream on the way out means you'll be fighting the current (and perhaps the wind, which can dog you no matter which way you head) on the way home. On the other hand, traveling downstream enables you to dock near a playground for some added terra firma fun. From the perspective of scenery, however, the two directions are pretty similar.

KID-FRIENDLY EATS: Sandwiches and bagels are on the menu at **Bruegger's Bagels** (739 Beacon St., tel. 617/630–9715). By contrast, **Blue Ribbon Barbecue** (1375 Washington St., West Newton, tel. 617/332–2583) dishes up authentic southern fare. There are only 12 stools inside, but on a nice canoeing day, you can get take-out and enjoy it in the great outdoors.

CHILDREN'S MUSEUM OF BOSTON

Most kids would classify the term "science playground" as an oxymoron (that is, if they could define the term "oxymoron"). But that's not the case at this children's museum, where the seemingly mundane is turned into magic. A fixture on the Boston scene for more than 80 years, this much-loved institution first achieved fame as one of the original interactive utopias. Today's version, in a roomy building not far from the Financial District, more than lives up to its pedigree.

Three floors of activities can keep a family busy for hours. At the aforementioned Science Playground, kids (and their scientifically challenged parents) get a handle on some laws of nature by playing with soap bubbles or ball mazes. At the Giant's Desk, a longtime favorite, comparatively lilliputian kids can take shelter in a behemoth pencil holder. For the other side of the size spectrum (i.e., miniatures), head to the extensive collection of dollhouses in the Hall of Toys. Today's globally oriented kids can play clerk or shopper in the Spanish-theme Supermercado, while children of the '60s can wax nostalgic in Grandma's House, whose period decor includes a Formica kitchen table and a black-and-white TV. Play

KEEP IN MIND: Cost-conscious parents (and who isn't!) can take advantage of Friday's extended museum hours (5–9), when admission is $1 for all. The only down side is that you'll likely have to deal with larger-than-normal crowds. The museum's other down side at any time is its size. Count on running yourself a little ragged to keep up with your children here (though you'll at least be having fun!) and relishing that much-deserved glass of wine (hot cocoa for the kids) when you get home.

300 Congress St.

 617/426–8855 recording,
617/426–6500 voice

 $7 ages 16 and up, $6
children 2–15, $2 age 1;
F 5–9 $1

 Sa–Th 10–5, F 10–9

 12 and under

vintage games in grandma's living room, or wend your way upstairs into the attic, where old trunks are full of dress-up clothes that kids can actually put on.

Newer additions include Arthur's World, where, thanks to the magic of blue-screen technology, you can appear on a monitor alongside the world's most famous aardvark, and Teen Tokyo, with a subway that seems to be in motion.

School-age children go wild here, scaling the newfangled climbing sculpture, sawing and hammering away at Johnny's Workbench, and exploring the below-sea-level world in Under the Dock. But little ones need not be left out; tots have their own special haven in the Play Space, a quiet, cozy spot with soft blocks, books, train sets, and crafts projects that's perfect on a weekday afternoon.

HEY, KIDS! How different is it to live in Japan? Find out by poking your head into the authentic Japanese house on the museum's third floor (you can look but not enter). The tatami mats (for sleeping) will probably fascinate kids used to a traditional American bed.

KID-FRIENDLY EATS: A **McDonald's** (316 Congress St., tel. 617/482–1746) is "conveniently" attached to the museum. The bad news (beyond the effect on your cholesterol) is that the interior connection takes you through a gift shop. Wise parents take a short detour outside. On weekdays, enjoy salads or made-to-order sandwiches at **Bethany's** (332 Congress St., tel. 617/423–4042); there are a few indoor tables, or eat outside by the museum. In late spring and summer, pick up snacks from the nearby **Milk Bottle,** aptly named for its shape. A short hike away, have your pick of eats at Fanueil Hall (see below).

COMMUNITY BOATING

I mages of Boston somehow don't seem complete without a picture of college crews sculling along the Charles River. The famed waterway, with the city as its backdrop, is a focal point of athletic pastimes. The banks teem with runners and bladers (*see* Dr. Paul Dudley White Bike Path), the water with oarsmen.

True, your kids may be too young to suit up with the Harvard crew team, but family sailing opportunities are available through this nonprofit organization. Wannabe Popeyes can sign up for a visitor pass ($50) that nets unlimited sailing time and craft rental for you and three guests for two consecutive days, provided the helmsman can pass muster with the staff here first. Those without experience will have to plan ahead and sign up for the 45-day membership that includes lessons. The cost is still reasonable ($75 per student), and once you've passed, you're in business to take the family along for the ride.

Less-experienced sailors might opt for a 14-foot Mercury boat, which accommodates up to four. More-experienced sailors can choose from sophisticated crafts that run up to about

KEEP IN MIND: Once you've paid your membership, there is no additional rental fee for the boats. Lessons are held regularly throughout the week; call for a schedule. If you're really enthusiastic, ask about rates (still very reasonable) for longer memberships. Experienced scullers can rent shells through Charles River Canoe and Kayak (*see above*), which also rents canoes for the Charles River Basin and other locations. For a guided cruise down the Charles, try Charles River Boat Company (100 Cambridgeside Pl., tel. 617/621–3001).

21 David Mugar Way (near Hatch Shell)

 $50 for 2 days of sailing

 Apr–Oct, M–F 1–sunset, Sa–Su 9–sunset

617/523–1038

5 and up; sailors 10 and up

22 feet. Boats launch from the Community Boating dock near the Longfellow Bridge and sail between it and the Massachusetts Avenue Bridge (the area commonly known as the basin). Kayaks and Windsurfers are available under the same membership; you'll have to pass muster for these as well.

Daily boat rentals have no time limit; you just have to be back by sunset. On busy days, however, the staff may ask you to check in hourly to ensure that there's no waiting list (this may be a good time to bring along that cell phone so you don't have to keep returning to the dock). If you're unsure whether you qualify as "experienced," do yourself a favor and check your status out before sail day, thus avoiding disappointing wails of "But you pro-o-o-omised."

KID-FRIENDLY EATS: The tasty Asian cuisine at the **King & I** (145 Charles St., tel. 617/227–3320) has made the restaurant a popular local haunt. American bistro fare at **Harvard Gardens** (316 Cambridge St., tel. 617/523–2727) includes comfort food as well as some more creative dishes.

HEY, KIDS! Want to be a sailor yourself? If you're age 10–18, you can join the summer Junior Program. From late June to late August, $1 buys all the lessons and watercraft rental you want for the season (certain hours apply). The program attracts 1,200 kids each year, but since attendance is staggered and there's a big fleet, getting a boat generally isn't a problem. To become a member, you must fill out an application, obtain parental permission, and show proof of your swimming capabilities.

COMMUNITY SOLAR SYSTEM TRAIL

T alk about a walking tour that's out of this world! Kids who turn their noses up at the Freedom Trail just might be lured into doing Boston on foot thanks to this novel tour. Best of all, in addition to walking, you'll be able to explore outer space by navigating some inner space (subway tunnels), too.

The tour is the creation of the folks at the Museum of Science. The sun, the hub of this solar system, is at the museum, while the nine planets (eight and a big rock, if you're persnickety about the designation of Pluto) are spread around the Boston area. Each bronze planet model is placed the appropriate relative distance from the sun. Your children's mission is to find each celestial body, make a rubbing in their official passport of the planet's symbol on the model (use pen, pencil, or crayon, as markers won't work), and bring home the passport with a mark for each.

The first five planets are easily accessible by foot or T. In addition to the sun, Mercury and Venus are located in the museum. Getting to Earth, at the Royal Sonesta Hotel,

HEY, KIDS!

The T is an old, but speedy, form of travel—in this case, interplanetary travel. Introduced in 1897, trains go up to 30 mph. Back then, rides cost a whopping 5¢; today it's up to 85¢, a small price to pay to get to Pluto.

KID-FRIENDLY EATS: Stop after Mars at the **Cambridgeside Galleria** (100 Cambridgeside Pl., tel. 617/621–8666). In addition to a traditional food court, there's a **Houlihan's** (tel. 617/577–1660), serving better-than-average chain fare. There's also plenty of food at a **food court** at South Station (Jupiter). At **Full Moon** (344 Huron Ave., Cambridge, tel. 617/354–6699), after Saturn, you'll find not only mouth-watering Mediterranean specialties but also a play room. The kids' hot dog/fries combo comes with carrots, and there's m&c and green beans, too. *Also see* the Museum of Science.

will take you about 10 minutes on foot. Mars is across the street at the Cambridgeside Galleria, and Jupiter is on the Red Line at South Station. Saturn, Uranus, and Neptune (in Cambridge, Jamaica Plain, and Saugus, respectively) are a little trickier. None requires a rocket to reach it, but you may need a combo of T and bus (or a car). Pluto is a straight shot from downtown, but it's way out in Newton (fittingly, the last stop on the Riverside Green Line), the equivalent of about 4.6 billion miles from the sun. Remember that you'll eventually need to get home, so though it may not be the most adventurous transportation, it's probably easier to just drive to Saugus.

When your family has reached every orb, mail the completed passport to the museum. You'll be rewarded with a certificate marking your accomplishment.

KEEP IN MIND: Like any interplanetary navigator, you'll want to map out your voyage beforehand, perhaps opting for the most convenient, rather than strict numerical, planetary order. There's also no rule that says you have to visit all alien worlds in one day. And if you follow the tour in reverse, you'll end up at the Museum of Science and its Welcome to the Universe exhibit. Passports can be downloaded from the Internet (Welcome to the Universe section at Mos.org) or picked up at the planetarium; either way, you'll get specific directions, parking information, and open hours for each site.

CURIOUS CREATURES KID'ZOO

Y ou might call this place a petting zoo with attitude. No fuzzy barnyard here, this indoor tropical rain forest houses a jungle full of exotic critters, including baby alligators, snakes, iguanas, and tarantulas. It's a small place, perhaps too small for some older kids, but it offers a rare opportunity to get up close and personal with some mighty unusual specimens.

Creatures line every corner of the structure. Birds fly overhead, a macaw squawks, and large turtles swim around happily in open-air ponds. First-time visitors are often agog at the site of enormous iguanas crawling free on the rafters above their heads. Thankfully, the more intimidating species (tarantulas and alligators, for example) are kept in roomy enclosures. If you think your kids won't want to visit with the hairy spider (talk about a face only a mother could love), think again. Even kids who cry for help at the sight of an arachnid in their basement are fascinated by this oversize creepy crawly. Those who'd like to touch will need to talk to a staff member; the ultra-helpful folks can be identified by either their iguana T-shirts or the presence of a live snake or bird draped about their person.

KEEP IN MIND: Animal-loving kids will want to spend a while here, so make sure you're comfortable. That means dress for the heat; in winter, layer sweaters over short sleeves and tank tops, and even sweatpants over shorts. If your kids need to flex their fingers afterward, try **Volcano Park** (Newbury St., tel. 978/536–5123), next door, or **Bonkers** (535 Lowell St., tel. 978/535–8355), both arcades.

168 Newbury St. (U.S. 1, south of Lowell St.), Peabody

978/535-5518

 $6

W-Th 10-6, F-Sa 10-7, Su 12-5

2-12

To be sure, your proximity to these unusual beasts (the animals, not the staff members) is pretty amazing, but equally impressive is the setting. Thick greenery and hanging vines effectively create a jungle look, and dim lights set the mood. Not content to have the place simply look like a jungle, owner Dean Kosch made it feel like a jungle, too—right down to the smell and the steamy heat. The place is a humid 80+° every day of the year, so you can kiss your good hair day good-bye.

Those concerned about animal rights can feel comfortable here. Kosch rescues all of the zoo's inhabitants from either inappropriate homes (would you believe someone actually kept an alligator as a pet?) or abandonment, and all are well-loved.

HEY, KIDS! Resident alligators live on a diet of rats. But how to keep a supply handy? Why, freeze them, of course! Just call it a ratsicle. The macaw lives on a much more civilized diet of fruit, seeds, and food pellets, but for occasional treats, he gets pizza and french fries.

KID-FRIENDLY EATS: You'll know you've reached the **Hilltop Steak House** (855 Broadway, Saugus, tel. 781/233-7700) when you spot the huge cows on the front lawn. You'll have to drive about 15 minutes (toward Boston) to get here, but the kitschy place is a local institution for steaks. The animals on the walls talk at **Bugaboo Creek** (Northshore Mall, tel. 978/538-0100), where chain fare includes steaks, salads, and a children's menu.

DAVIS FARMLAND

T he phone number here spells "MOOO"; the fax spells "OINK." Need you ask how much Farmer Davis likes his livestock?

After more than 100 years of farming this acreage, the Davis family—father John and sons Larry and Doug—have found a new way to use their spread, namely reinventing it as a children's discovery farm. Sure, there's a little "moo, moo" here and an "oink, oink" there to listen to, but this is also an interactive adventure. The real treat is not just what your kids will see and hear, but what they'll get to do: feeding, milking, and some plain old-fashioned cuddling.

Farm residents include the usual suspects: your basic sheep, goats, pigs, and cows. (Most of the grown-ups are in pens, but some of the babies delight kids by wandering around their feet.) In addition, however, the Davis enterprise features some truly rare and unusual critters: Gloucester Old Spot Pigs, long-haired Highland Cattle, and Tamworth Pigs, to name a few. Most folks are surprised to find farm animals on the endangered species

KID-FRIENDLY EATS: Corny? Sure. But the on-site **Herd Rock Calfe** is also pretty cute, serving up yummy burgers, dogs, and PB & Js. Thoughtful extras include baby food. For traditional Americana, try **Barbers Crossing North** (175 Leominster Rd., tel. 978/422–8438).

KEEP IN MIND: Activities at the farm, such as egg collecting (some of the chickens lay multicolor eggs) and cow and goat milking, occur at specified times throughout the day. Check for a schedule on the way in. Pony rides ($2 extra) are also available. In summer, ask about special events featuring carnival-style performers. If you have older *and* younger children, you might want to buy a discounted combination pass for the farm and the Davis Mega Maze (*see below*), across the street.

145 Redstone Hill Rd.
(off Rte. 62), Sterling

978/422-6666

$7.50 ages 2 and up

Mid-Apr–Labor Day, daily 9:30–4:30;
early Sept–Oct, Th–Su 9:30–4:30

6 and under

list, but these are. In fact, the main part of the Davis business is finding—and, in many cases, successfully breeding—such imperiled beasts, some of whose numbers have dwindled to mere hundreds.

That the discovery section is only a small portion of the 230-acre farm was part of a well-thought-out plan. Fathers themselves, the farmers understood the difficulty of trying to keep track of a wandering toddler or two. The discovery farm provides enough activities to entertain a young child in a space small enough (about 375 feet from center to edge) and well-enough designed (landings rise up as you walk outward, increasing visibility) to allow parents to stay in one place while seeing nearly the whole area. To view the rest of the spread, take a spin on one of the tractor-pulled hayrides or enjoy the fresh air in the sand, water, or climbing play areas.

HEY, KIDS! What is that funky-looking creature with the long, wooly hair and the donkey ears? That is a Patou—Pete the Patou, to be exact—a rare donkey from France. The odd-but-loveable animal used to be bred with a specific type of horse to create a kind of super mule, which was used to haul heavy items through the mountains. Alas, the popularity of motors made this off-spring—and the Patous themselves—largely unnecessary. Pete is one of just a few of his kind left in the world.

DAVIS MEGA MAZE

46

T he sign says "Welcome," but it might just as well say "Get Lost!" That, after all, is the whole point of this confounding creation—to enter the sprawling tangle of corn plants and see how long it takes you to get out. Think it's a piece of cake? Think again.

Carved out of a 6-acre field of corn, the Davis maze has more than 3 miles of paths to navigate, with plants that tower as high as 10 feet and an elaborate sound system that keeps things lively. The average visitor takes 45 minutes–1½ hours to get to the other side. "The parents always joke on the way in about racing through and coming back later for the kids," muses Larry Davis, who, along with dad, John, and brother Doug, owns the farmland the maze is on. "But it's always the kids who make it out first."

Designed by renowned English maze maker Adrian Fisher, the Davis labyrinth takes on a new form each year. Previous designs have included dragons and Blackbeard (from above, it really looked like a pirate). Inside, paths wind in every which direction. Fisher even adds a three-dimensional feature: bridges that can be crossed over and under.

KEEP IN MIND: Don't underestimate the maze's scope. It's absolutely not for people with claustrophobia or frail health. If you really must leave, find a staff member at any of the maze's bridges, and he or she will lead you out pronto. To avoid the need for an un-timely exit, use the bathroom first; as the brochure says, "there's a portable toilet inside, but you'll have to find it." Also think ahead (and call) if there's been rain. Heavy downpours can create corn soup that closes the maze for a day or so. And the best plan with children 3 and under? Bring a backpack.

Since the maze opened in 1998, some visitors have become very creative (or perhaps desperate), arriving equipped with cell phones and walkie-talkies. "It doesn't help," Davis says with a smile. Inside, staff members are on hand to give good-natured (and always on-the-level) prompts, such as "If I were you, I'd turn right." Don't despair if you do need some help; 90% of the guests here do. If you know you're going to have trouble, you can opt to carry a 10-foot flag; wave it around, and a staff member will appear at your side. Don't have a flag? Just look confused. The staff is instructed to offer help to those who appear to need it.

KID-FRIENDLY EATS: The Davises keep a **grill** going with hot dogs and hamburgers and carry those all-important beverages. The **Country Fare II Restaurant** (27 Main St., tel. 978/422– 9779) features home-cooked favorites from burgers to seafood, as well as kid stuff; don't miss the homemade pies and sweets.

HEY, KIDS! You'll probably be ready to go into the maze again even before mom and dad get out the first time (admission includes unlimited trips through), but it doesn't have to be the same adventure twice. It's possible to get to the end by crossing every bridge—or none at all. Set a different course for yourself, and see how much longer (or shorter) it takes.

DISCOVERY MUSEUMS

I t's not hard to figure out what parents like about this homespun spot north of Boston. You certainly could find showier places, but for pure indoor exploration value, this duo is worth gold.

Two buildings make for one giant discovery. Up front, a cozy renovated Victorian house shelters the Children's Discovery Museum, for younger kids. Ten theme rooms span three floors, all filled with toys to fuel the imagination. The smell of soap bubbles permeates the Water Discovery room, where kids can dive into buckets of water for bubble play (in the figurative sense, thank you). Wall-size chalkboards let mural artists go to town; they can also make sidewalk masterpieces on the driveway outside. Lush (painted-on) greenery and props in the Safari and Jungle rooms are perfect places to go wild. Bessie's Play Diner has old-style booths, counter, stools, and plenty of cooking utensils and "food," and in this kitchen, parents get to be waited on for a change.

HEY, KIDS!
Don't overlook those giant satellite dishes outside. They're not for TV reception but instead can help you discover the strange ways that sound travels. Stand at one while a friend stands at the other. Now take turns whispering. How well can you hear each other?

KEEP IN MIND: Staff at the Children's Discovery Museum strive to keep it from getting too cozy, meaning at busy times, you may have to wait to get in. Entry is staggered through the use of numbers (like at the deli), but here you can grab a number, leave, and come back. Don't fret if your number is called while you're gone; you'll still be admitted on the spot. Rainy days and Thursday afternoon story times are often busy, so come early. Entry to the larger Science Discovery Museum is usually not a problem. To spot the place, look for the giant dinosaur outside.

177 Main St. (near Rte. 2), Acton

  Mid-June–early Sept, T–Su 9–4:30; early Sept–mid-June, T and Th–F 1–4:30, W 9–6, Sa–Su 9–4:30

 978/264-4201 $6 1 museum, $9 both ages 1 and up   Children's Discovery Museum 1–6, Science Discovery Museum 6–12

Out back, the newer Science Discovery Museum is designed for schoolkids. Two stories house dozens of science experiments to push, pull, stomp, and roll. Traditional wares include magnet play, pendulums, and recyclable crafts, to name only three, or see if you can manipulate a Ping-Pong ball using just the airflow from a blow dryer. Some exhibits are purely visual: The enormous box of bread tags (those little plastic things that hold the bread bag closed) gives a quantitative handle on the concept of "1 million" (it's astounding). Activities aside, the science center's greatest achievement is layout; there's enough to keep kids plenty busy without rendering them overwhelmed.

Dozens of books accompany activities at both museums, meaning tots can curl up with a story, and older kids can look up further information about the various sciences if their interest is piqued.

KID-FRIENDLY EATS: If your kids feel like making a new discovery in the food department, take them for some tasty Thai food up the street at **Benjarong Restaurant** (214 Main St., tel. 978/635-9580). If you must go for more standard fare, there's a **Friendly's** (387 Massachusetts Ave., tel. 978/263-0530) less than a mile away.

DR. PAUL DUDLEY WHITE BIKE PATH

44

One of the best things about Boston is the Charles River. The waterway is a focal point of boating activity, from the sailboats that dot the horizon in the summer to the Head of the Charles regatta in fall, which literally fills the basin with college crew teams. Devout landlubbers need not feel left out, however; there are plenty of vantage points to enjoy the goings on. Planners and landscape architects obviously thought carefully about how to maximize use of this picturesque river, installing miles of surrounding paved paths to accommodate those on foot, skates, and bicycle.

Twenty miles of path—named for a renowned local cardiologist—stretch from Prospect Street, near downtown Waltham, to the dam at Science Park. Sprinkled along the way are lots of park benches, fields, and public pools, as well as a number of well-equipped playgrounds.

The best-known paths are those closest to Boston. Trails travel both the Cambridge and Boston sides of the river, but you'll be wise to stick to the latter, as they are generally set

KEEP IN MIND: Come to Memorial Drive around April–October, when a section near Harvard Square is closed to cars 9–dusk. In May the Watertown Dam (above Galen Street) has a spectacular fish run (scads of herring come to breed); there's also a public swimming pool and spray pool. Another good ride, the 10½-mile Minuteman Commuter Rail, mirrors Paul Revere's ride. In-line skaters find nirvana 90 minutes away at the 20,000-square-foot, indoor Skater Island (1747 W. Main Rd., Middletown, RI, tel. 401/848–8078). Outdoors, try the new Reservation Road Skateboard Park (140 Reservation Rd., Hyde Park, tel. 617/635–4505).

Both sides of the Charles River, between Science Park and downtown Waltham

617/727-5114

 Free

 Daily sunrise–sunset

All ages

back a bit from the road. The Hatch Shell is a nice place for a rest (look for events during warmer months). You might also detour across the Larz Anderson Bridge to appreciate the funkiness of Harvard Square. But beware of traffic (bike, blade, and car) on the paths as well as at teeming crosswalks.

Those with young children are probably better off hitting the road farther west. At Artesani park (off Soldier's Field Road in Brighton), you'll find a great place for the kids (with new playground equipment) and a good place to stash your car while you ride. Farther upriver, a 2-mile loop west from Watertown Square and back again (travel between Galen and Bridge streets) is short on traffic and long on scenery. Taken together, the stretch from Artesani to Watertown plus the loop is about 6 miles, but it's all relatively flat—and mostly set away from the road—so even kids can travel at a good clip.

TRANSPORTATION: If you're planning on taking a train to your starting point (say, to Harvard Square) you'll need a bike permit. Bikes are permitted on the Blue, Red, and Orange lines as well as on the commuter rail, but not on the Green Line. There are a whole list of dos and don'ts, so call the MBTA (tel. 617/222–3200). If you're going to Watertown, you'll have to drive, as bikes are not allowed on buses.

KID-FRIENDLY EATS: Harvard Square's **Au Bon Pain** (1360 Massachusetts Ave., Cambridge, tel. 617/661–8738) has good chain fare and great people-watching, while **Brew Moon Restaurant & Microbrewery** (50 Church St., Cambridge, tel. 617/499–2739) has hearty pub fare. For kebabs with Greek flair, try **Demo's** (84 Mt. Auburn St., Watertown, tel. 781/924–9660).

DREAMS OF FREEDOM MUSEUM

Though New England is famous for early immigration (remember Plymouth Rock?), most people think of New York's Ellis Island when pondering latter-day arrivals. So it might come as a surprise that Boston is number two as a port of entry for immigrants, having welcomed more than 100,000 newcomers per year to American soil in the early 20th century.

Such is the hook of this newest addition to the Boston museum trail. Located on Benjamin Franklin's birth site (Franklin, for the record, was born here, but his father came from England), the 10,000-square-foot facility explores the path of immigrants—everything from how they came to what they brought. Though Old Ben's house burned down long ago, the site provides a historic spot to launch the adventure.

Far from giving just a flat retelling of old stories, the museum employs what the National Institute of Boston (the social services agency behind the museum) likes to refer to as "Disney-esque" touches, with high-tech wizardry designed to attract the attention

HEY, KIDS!

The Golden Stairs aren't from a fairy tale; they're real, once leading from the old (and long defunct) East Boston immigration station. Why they're called "golden" is the million- dollar question. One theory has it that the stairs' handrails shone gold in the afternoon sun.

KEEP IN MIND: In July and August, look for tours of the Immigrant Trail with costumed guides. Choose from Ben Franklin (portrayed by Emmy-winning actor Bill Meikle), Abigail Adams, or a fictional immigrant. The three-hour programs include walking tours and lunch at tony Maison Robert; for that reason (and the $35 price tag), these tours are definitely geared toward older children and adults. Meikle also performs "Ben Franklin's Colonial Cabaret" ($20) on Friday and Saturday nights in July and August. Call Historical Entertainments (tel. 781/648–0628) for a schedule.

1 Milk St.

 617/338-6022

 $7.50 ages 13 and up,
$3.50 children 3–12

 Daily 9:30–6

 10 and up

of today's high-tech generation. What that means is that you can expect to be immersed: A ship deck pitches, a gangplank moves, and walls whisper. Holographic "hosts" guide you through—there's even a holo-video Ben Franklin who plays master of ceremonies.

Artifacts, newspaper clippings, and photographs add to the picture, and you can wrap up your visit with a stint in a video booth, where you can add your own family story to the melting pot. Just record your name, digital image, and a three-minute narrative. Though the museum is designed for elementary schoolkids, there are enough bells and whistles to keep younger children busy, too. Want more exploration? Pick up a map detailing the Immigrant Trail, which starts with the Irish Famine Memorial right outside the museum's door. If the adventure has stirred your curiosity about genealogy, check with staff members about how to use the Internet to research your family tree.

KID-FRIENDLY EATS: Discover English culinary roots at the **Elephant & Castle** (161 Devonshire St., tel. 617/350–9977), a British pub featuring all the staples—shepherd's pie, bangers and mash, and fish-and-chips—as well as a full range of English beers for mom and dad. Weekdays, find good ol' American sandwiches and salads at the **Milk Street Cafe** (0 Post Office Sq., tel. 617/350–7275).

DRUMLIN FARM

Just a few minutes from the bustle of Boston, this sizable working farm provides a bucolic respite for kids in the big city. More than 200 acres of farmland get worked throughout the year, and all the standard barnyard creatures are here, accompanied by their respective sound effects.

The heart of the operation, the Farm Core, is a short walk from the entrance. This is where you'll find the classic red barn as well as a chicken coop and pigsty. The cast of livestock includes milking cows, goats, draft horses, great big pigs that look very happy in dirt, and a couple of noisy roosters roaming around free. Watch out for impromptu vocal performances by these guys! Though Drumlin is not a petting zoo, it offers frequent demonstrations (e.g., cow milking) that get you up close to some of the animals. On occasion, you can even enter the chicken room and gather eggs. (Plan on purchasing the eggs you collect.)

Beyond the central farm, five trails lead to remote fields and pastures. Keep your eyes open; you may spot a fox, coyote, rabbit, or weasel—as well as some rescued animals and

KEEP IN MIND: Baby-animal lovers will want to come in spring, when mamas-to-be are ready to have their little ones. Chicks generally start arriving around the end of March or beginning of April; lambs arrive from late February to early March. Public programs, including cow milking and animal education, are held daily in season, weekends only from November to March. Hayrides operate daily April–November (extra charge). Call for recorded information about the day's activities.

birds housed in habitats near the Farm Core. Walk to the top of the drumlin, the glacial deposit the farm is named for, and be rewarded with some great views. On a clear day, you can see all the way to Mt. Wackiest. Stroller-pushers will have to stick to the main paved roads, except in summer, when the dirt paths tend to dry out enough for wheels to pass.

One word of warning: The animals' cute and cuddly appearances mask some harsh realities of farming, namely meat production. The freezer at the entrance advertising farm-fresh pork and beef may engender questions. Parents of young children should be prepared for some discussion.

HEY, KIDS! How does a chicken chew without teeth? The secret is in the feed. Chicken chow includes hard material made of ground oyster shells. The bits of grit help grind the food in the birds' gizzard, part of their digestive tract.

KID-FRIENDLY EATS: Open March–December, **Dairy Joy** (331 North Ave., Weston, tel. 781/894–7144) is one of those much-loved neighborhood spots where you can enjoy sandwiches, burgers, and ice cream alfresco. Year-round, you can sit inside and dine on Italian food at **Racine's** (Rte. 117, Concord, tel. 978/371–3280).

ECOTARIUM

You have to hand it to the folks who named the EcoTarium (formerly called the New England Science Center). It may be a made-up word (then again, "on-line" wasn't in the dictionary once), but the bon mot perfectly describes this interactive science exploratory dedicated entirely to studying the environment. On 60 acres of wooded land, the EcoTarium uses all of its wares to convey its message. Indoor exhibits explain about our environment; outdoor exhibits actually let you explore it.

Half the adventures take place in the three-story exhibit hall. Here's where you can explore different ecosystems (such as a simulated soil tunnel you can climb inside) and learn about earth's creatures great and small. In the MicroDiner, microscopes reveal what might be taking up residence in pond water or your kitchen cabinets (you'll never look at expired grocery items the same way again).

What keeps the EcoTarium from being just another science center is its resident wildlife. Working as a rescue facility, the institution houses dozens of animals—from bald eagles

KID-FRIENDLY EATS: Indoor vending machines provide all-important snacks. In warm weather, the outdoor **grill** sells hamburgers, hot dogs, and the like. For a bigger selection, take Route 9 to **East Side Marios** (79 Boston Tpke., Shrewsbury, 508/755–0900). The Italian eatery has everything from pizza to seafood.

KEEP IN MIND: Major renovations have spiffed up the 175-year-old place, so if you haven't visited in a while, expect improvements. Changing programs include story times, puppet shows, and craft activities. Those ages 7 and up can take a guided tour of the Tree Canopy Walkway. The structure takes you 40 feet up into the trees, just like field researchers. You'll have to learn the ropes first—literally—as participants are secured by ropes. Call and ask about dates, times, and fees. Another popular feature is the 15-minute ride on the narrow-gauge Explorer Express Train.

222 Harrington Way (Massachusetts Tpke. Exit 11), Worcester

 508/929-2700

 $7 ages 17 and up, $5 children 3–16

 M–Sa 10–5, Su 12–5

 3–12

to polar bears—all of whom have been injured or abandoned. "All of our animals have a story," says a staff member. Some will be released back into the wild; others, due to injury or socialization problems, will reside here permanently. You can visit with small critters—field mice, a tiny saw-whet owl, and a python, among others—in the exhibit hall. Larger and more exotic animals are housed outside along the two self-guided nature trails: the Timescape Trail and the Lower Loop Trail. When you've had enough active investigation, take a seat at the new pavilion on the serene pond and revel in watching the world around you.

And if our world is too confining, explore the universe beyond by attending a show at the on-site planetarium or one of the occasional night-sky watches that uses the EcoTarium's high-powered telescopes (extra charge for both).

HEY, KIDS! What's a python's favorite dish? Live mouse. That may seem impossible given their seemingly tiny mouths, but they manage. In order to open wide, the slithery guys have mastered the art of dislocating their bottom jaw, enabling them to consume their prey whole. If you're "lucky" (luck being a relative thing), you might get to observe the resident python having dinner. Prospective snake owners, take note: The huge creature here started out as someone's small pet.

EDAVILLE RAILROAD

40

E llis Atwood probably never expected his Christmas tradition to get quite this big. A cranberry farmer, Atwood used his narrow-gauge railroad—originally purchased to transport berries—as a sort of living holiday card, taking friends for scenic rides around his brightly Christmas-lit farm. Word got out about the excursions, and lo and behold, a business was born.

Christmas rail rides stayed a tradition at the Atwood farm until 1991, when the proprietors shut them down (Atwood had since died). Nine years later, new owners came on board, restoring the sheen of the old engines and relaunching them into service.

Though Atwood's original vision was for Christmas excursions only, today you can board the trains much of the year. Scenic trips around the 1,800-acre property (a roughly 5½-mile circuit) take about 30 minutes, with passengers chugging along in vintage box cars behind turn-of-the-20th-century engines. The current crop of trains rely solely on diesel power, but there are plans for the addition of a vintage steam engine. Trains are stationed

KEEP IN MIND: If you want to learn more about the business of cranberries, head over to Ocean Spray Cranberry World (158 Water St., Plymouth, tel. 508/747–2350). The center details the history of the cranberry from Native American days until now and offers a tasting of 10 different types of juices. Cranberry World is open daily, roughly mid–May through November; admission is free. Labor Day through October, South Carver is also home to the medieval antics of King Richard's Faire (Rte. 58, Carver, tel. 508/866–5391).

7 Eda Ave. (Rte. 58, off I–495),
South Carver

508/866–8190 or
800/877–EDAVILLE

$12.50 ages 13 and up,
$7.50 children 3–12

June–Oct, daily 10–5; Nov–early Jan,
M–F 4–9, Sa–Su 2–9

All ages

at Edaville's Victorian-style village, where a railroad theme park also includes an antique carousel, petting zoo, nature trails, a kids' club with climb-on farm equipment, and two permanently derailed cabooses peddling ice cream and candy. A $5 million rehab, begun by the new owners, promises to polish the place to a nostalgic glow.

Still, the highlight of a visit here is unquestionably the train ride. Autumn riders can witness the cranberry harvest—watching as the flooded bogs become crimson with floating berries—and, around Veterans' Day, the farm becomes the site of World War II reenactments. Later, the ongoing Christmas tradition returns, featuring elaborate lights as well as an ice palace sculpture, a huge gingerbread house, and a visit from that jolly old fellow from the north.

KID-FRIENDLY EATS: The railroad theme park has a brand new **cafeteria** with all the essentials (sandwiches, salads, snacks). At Christmas, you'll also find warm cider and other treats. **Cornerstone's** (96 N. Main St., Carver, tel. 508/866–2665) is known for its bar-and-grill fare.

HEY, KIDS: There was no Presidents' Day back in the 17th century (not surprising, since there was no president), not to mention no Veterans', Memorial, and Martin Luther King, Jr. days, so children had to find other ways to get out of school. Fortunately, there were cranberries. Back in those days, the little red fruit was so important that at harvest time, schoolhouses (and businesses) were shut down so that everyone could help.

FANUEIL HALL

I t's the plight of the Boston-area newcomer to be confounded by local monikers that don't sound like they're spelled. Hence tourists routinely ask for Fan-wheel or Fan-oil Hall (the proper pronunciation is either Fan-yuhl or Fan-uhl). Equally confusing is that Fanueil Hall does not actually refer to the larger retail area with which it's often confused—the attached Quincy (pronounced Quin-zy) Market—but rather just to the historic Great Hall itself, the nation's first public town meeting house.

Built in 1742 by Peter Fanueil, the hall acquired the nickname "Cradle of Liberty" after playing host to numerous meetings during which Colonists (verbally) blasted the British. Organizers of the Boston Tea Party originally met here, but the gathering got so large that it had to reconvene in the Old South Meeting House. The hall's modern-day legacy includes the launch of presidential candidacies for John F. Kennedy and Michael Dukakis.

Today Fanueil Hall retains its status as a multipurpose meet-and-greet spot, but most modern gatherers come sporting an ice cream cone (Steve's, in Quincy Market, is an

HEY, KIDS!

Check out the grasshopper weather vane atop the Great Hall. The oversize *locustidae* (the insect family that includes the grasshopper) has symbolized the port of Boston since the 1600s. Of many legends surrounding it, one has it that it was a wealthy London merchant's good luck charm and was borrowed by Fanueil.

KID-FRIENDLY EATS: The question isn't where to eat here, but how much.

Slightly surly service is part of the charm at **Durgin Park** (340 Fanueil Hall Marketplace, tel. 617/227–2038). Enormous portions of steak, seafood, and other fare are often accompanied by long waits. Inside the Quincy Market building, take your pick of a couple dozen vendors, from **Philadelphia Steak & Hoagie** (tel. 617/742–4773) and the Greek **Mykonos Fair** (tel. 617/742–8349) to tons of delicious bake shops.

0 Fanueil Hall Sq.

 617/635-3105

 Free

Great Hall daily 9–5; Marketplace M–Sa, 10–9, Su 12–6;
Quincy Market's restaurants and pubs open late

All ages

absolute must!) or a latte rather than an agenda. The Great Hall itself is one of the few historic buildings that you can still enter free of charge, although it may be closed during special events. Daily 15-minute talks by park rangers (every half hour) detail the building's history, and revolutionary weaponry is on display in the Museum of the Ancient and Honorable Artillery Company, on the fourth floor.

For those too young to appreciate the historic majesty, the area also boasts daily street performances during fair-weather months, roughly March–October. The jugglers, storytellers, musicians, and other entertainers here are some of the country's best and are often hilarious.

Sadly (for parents' wallets, anyway), the historic landmark is surrounded by Quincy Market's shrine to retail. Those who must have a new Boston souvenir will find the place brimming with knickknacks as well as more high-end merchandise—a far cry from what Sam Adams envisioned.

KEEP IN MIND: With roughly 40 acts, there's bound to be performers any summer day. Special events take place for St. Patrick's Day and during the winter holidays, too. You can get a schedule of events and street performers by calling the Fanueil Hall Events Line (tel. 617/523–1300). Twenty-minute horse-and-carriage tours (for hire at North and Clinton streets) are another old-fashioned, albeit pricey ($35), diversion. On Congress Street, look for the graceful Holocaust memorial, and a few blocks in the other direction, let kids run off steam at the waterside Christopher Columbus Park.

FENWAY PARK TOUR

You can't grow up in Boston without knowing about the Green Monster, a fixture in these parts since 1912. Unlike most ogres, however, this one doesn't torment children in pajamas, but rather grown men in pin-stripe pants.

The monster, of course, is not a "who" but a "what." Towering 37 feet, the enormous green left-field wall is compensation for Fenway Park's diminutive size (only 310 feet from home plate to left). To get up close to the monster, your kids will either have to play outfield for a Major League ball club (provided Fenway is still standing then) or take one of the hourly 50-minute guided tours, which tell about Red Sox history and provide access to key spots within this fabled landmark.

The tour reveals all sorts of Fenway lore: about the greats who've played here, Babe Ruth and Ted Williams included; that the park was named for its neighborhood (the Fens), not the other way around; about the 1920 trade of Babe Ruth to the Yankees, resulting in the

KID-FRIENDLY EATS: If you're not planning to stay for a game and chow down on lots of concession food, head over to **Pizzeria Uno** (1 Brookline Ave., tel. 617/262–4911), which has the chain's exceptional pizza plus some tasty Italian salads and pastas. If you're up for an active meal, **Jillian's** (145 Ipswich St., tel. 617/437–0300) is a local institution offering pub grub and a building full of arcade games.

4 Yawkey Way

617/267-9440

 $5 ages 13 and up, $3 children 12 and under

May–Sept, M–F 10–1, also 2 on non-game days

8 and up

infamous "curse of the Bambino"; and the reason for the net above the monster, to protect pedestrians on Lansdown Street.

Sights on the tour include the press level (command central), where the organ music and public addresses originate; the premium 600-Club seats; and a private luxury box, available only on some tours. But the moment of moments comes when you step down on field level. You won't be able to round the bases, but you can walk on the warning track, getting close enough to the Green Monster to "hug it, kiss it, and throw yourself against it," as one guide put it. (You're simply asked not to leave any dirty fingerprints—or tears.) And there's nothing like the vantage point you get from a seat in the Red Sox dugout. The only thing that's missing is one of those greasy vendor sausages. For that, you'll have to come to a game and sit in the stands.

HEY, KIDS! How's your knowledge of Morse code? The dots and dashes on the Big Green Monster actually spell something. Can you figure out what it is? (Guides give the answer near the end of the tour).

KEEP IN MIND: Fenway's nook in the city keeps it from expanding its capacity—and hence its profitability—beyond the current 33,871 seats. That means the adored (or abhorred, depending on your team allegiance) icon is a likely candidate for replacement. The moral of the story for wanna-be Fenway tourists: Don't put off 'til tomorrow... Reservations for the tour are highly recommended.

FRANKLIN PARK ZOO

L ong the Rodney Dangerfield of the zoological community—for years locals asserted that it was the worst zoo in the country—the Franklin Park Zoo has been experiencing something of a renaissance of late. Those who haven't visited in a while are in for a surprise.

Lowland gorillas in the Tropical Forest are just a few of the star residents of this urban zoo, now a much happier animal home thanks to recent attention. Several hundred creatures make up today's zoo community, including zebras, primates, leopards, exotic birds (even a couple of peacocks strutting around free), and numerous slithery reptiles. Ndugu and Mafuta—two African lions—live happily in their Kalahari Kingdom, while a couple of long-necked neighbors dwell in the Giraffe Savannah. Zookeepers are adding some panache by creating natural habitats (an image hampered by the sight of apartment buildings beyond the endangered Bactrian camel habitat). The lion home, while on the small side, is indeed reminiscent of terrain the big cats might inhabit in Africa. Lots of large-pane windows give clear views of the felines, and props, including bleached animal bones and a Jeep wedged halfway inside the habitat, are effective scene setters. (To feel like you're on

HEY, KIDS!
Snow leopards can leap 15 to 20 feet— straight up—in a single bound. That's about equivalent to the height of a 1½- to 2-story building. Take that, Superman.

KEEP IN MIND: The good news about visiting in winter is that you'll encounter fewer people (you didn't come to see them anyway); the bad news is that you won't see the giraffes (they're housed in their barn from November to March) or the butterflies. Zoo New England, the private, nonprofit company that operates this zoo, also runs the **Stone Zoo** (Pond St., Stoneham, tel. 781/438–5100), which has not been the bene-factor of a renovation, though changes are under way. Rhode Island has an outstanding zoo: Roger Williams Park Zoo (1000 Elmwood Ave., Providence, tel. 401/785–3510).

1 Franklin Park Rd.

 $7 ages 16 and up,
$4 children 2-15

Apr–Sept, M–F 10–5, Sa–Su 10–6;
Oct–Mar, daily 10–4

617/541–5466

 All ages

safari, look through the Jeep's windshield.) Wallabies and kangaroos inhabit the outback of the Bongo Congo Trail, and in the aforementioned Tropical Forest, you'll find all the primates, including a scene-stealing baby gorilla born in 1999. Large glassed-in areas were designed to give humans the best view, but those expressive faces staring back from the other side might make you wonder exactly who's watching whom.

Acres of wide, flat paths make the zoo a particular favorite for families with young children who need to run. Look for additional kid-attention-grabbers to be added in the near future, including a sizeable farmyard with a "contact corral," where you'll find the expected (goat, sheep, etc.) as well as a few unexpected barn dwellers, such as owls and snakes.

KID-FRIENDLY EATS: The number of dining options depends on the season. During warm weather, the **Kalahari Kitchen** offers fresh pizza, snacks, and drinks, whereas the **Outback Barbecue** has grilled chicken and burgers. The **Giddy-Up Grill,** the only zoo eatery open year-round, features burgers, hot dogs, chicken tenders, and snacks as well as indoor and outdoor seating. Also see restaurants under the Blue Hills Trailside Museum and Reservation.

FREEDOM TRAIL

36

Kids who've grown up on video games and search engines may consider historic sightseeing the entertainment equivalent of brussels sprouts. But once they get walking the Freedom Trail, children may be surprised to find themselves actually having a good time.

This historic trail, created in 1958, links some of the area's most famous landmarks—living history style. Follow the red-lined path to the home of Paul Revere, where you can try on Colonial garb; the Old North Church (*see below*), where you can walk up to the loft where the famed lanterns were hung; and the Old South Meeting House, where defiant patriots conceived the idea for the Boston Tea Party. Most of the sites are free; others charge a nominal fee.

Experts recommend starting at Boston Common (*see above*). From there, the 2½-mile trail wends through Beacon Hill, downtown, and the North End before concluding in Charlestown. Highlights for most kids include the three burying grounds, such as the Granary, where you'll find headstones for such famous patriots as Paul Revere and Samuel Adams.

KEEP IN MIND: Call ahead to ask about seasonal abbreviated tours offered by the National Park Service (April 15 through November, roughly 1½ hours) and the Boston Park Rangers. Colonial costumed guides (tel. 617/227–8800) offer tours June through August and will also arrange private tours. Little Feet Tours (77 N. Washington St., tel. 617/367–3766) run tours for young children, and special ranger-led programs include the free Haunt Jaunt (minimum: 10 people), a scavenger hunt through the Granary Burying Ground.

Boston Common to the Bunker Hill Monument

 617/242-5642 National Park Service,
617/635-7383 Boston Park Rangers

 Trail free; some attractions charge

 Trail open 24 hrs; attraction hrs vary, most daily 9-5

8 and up

You can make the whole adventure (at least 4½ hours) into a badge-earning mission by picking up the free Junior Ranger Pack from either of the National Park Service visitor centers: downtown at 15 State Street (across from the Old State House) or at the Charlestown Navy Yard. Complete the activities and return them to either office for your official Junior Ranger Badge. Another kid-friendly activity is the park service's Hit the Trail Passport book ($2.95), which has a space for a stamp from every stop.

To save the tired dogs, hop either the water shuttle (Pier 4, $1 per person) back to downtown Boston or the Orange Line from the Community College station to the Back Bay.

KID-FRIENDLY EATS: Pause on your historical journey at the equally historical **Union Oyster House** (41 Union St., tel. 617/227-2750), America's oldest restaurant (1826). The tasty food includes seafood and grills. For a modern experience, hop the T to the **Hard Rock Cafe** (131 Clarendon St., tel. 617/424-7625).

HEY, KIDS! Legend has it that Mother Goose is buried in the Granary Burying Ground. Locals believe that Elizabeth Goose, who got her name from her husband, Isaac Goose (formerly VerGoose), was the famous storyteller. She is supposed to have concocted the rhymes to entertain her 20 children and stepchildren. Her grave lies on the north side of the burying ground (check map at the gate), but remember that rubbings are not allowed.

GEORGE'S ISLAND

If you're coming to George's Island for the first time, you may well wonder, "Who's George?" It's a good question. Though documents attribute the name to Capt. John George, historians disagree about whether the island's moniker actually predates the 18th-century Boston merchant (island records date back as far as 1690). Nevertheless, historic discord can't mar the island's inherent charms. Seven miles from downtown, the island of the mysterious George is one of the most popular—and serene—spots in Boston Harbor. Home to a 19th-century fort, the parcel of land combines the best parts of outdoor adventuring: fresh air, great views, and incomparable historic exploration.

Most notable is stately Ft. Warren, whose massive, 150-year-old granite walls stand about 30 feet high and 8 feet thick. The 10-acre military structure was used from the Civil War to the end of World War II. Unlike Ft. Warren's former "guests" (i.e., Confederate prisoners), today's visitors have their run of the place. You can storm the parade grounds (the grassy area inside fortress walls), climb into the two observation towers, and poke around the long-deserted casemates (living and artillery compartments) and abandoned gun

HEY, KIDS!

What the heck is a sallyport? The girlish name refers to a fort's main entrance (from the French for "leaving gate"). Other strange names include the demi-lune (the half-moon-shape building on the fort's north) and the scarp gallery (Bastion E), where musket-toting soldiers stood guard.

KEEP IN MIND: Water service to the island is provided from Hingham as well as Boston; ask Boston Harbor Cruises for details. You can also hop a free water taxi to some of the other islands in the Boston Harbor Island State Park/National Recreation Area (Peddock's, Lovell's, Grape, Bumpkin, and Gallops), but you'll have to return to George's to catch the boat home. During summer, free ranger-led fort tours are offered several times daily. Inquire at the information booth at the dock or with the Metropolitan District Commission (tel. 617/727–5290), which also provides information on summer Civil War re-enactments and other events.

Departures: 63 Long Wharf

 $8 ages 13 and up,
$6 children 3–12

Late Apr–mid-June, Sa–Su; mid-June–
mid-Oct, daily; depart hourly 10–5

 617/227–4321 Boston Harbor Cruises,
617/727–7676 Boston Harbor Island State Park

All ages

batteries. The truly observant might be able to discern the purpose of some compartments. Brick ovens, for example, signal that you're in the bakery; the small wood-lined rooms were probably powder magazines. You might even spot a remnant of combat—the purported impression of a cannonball—in a cracked walkway outside Bastion D. Also keep an eye out for the ghost of the lady in black. Historians declare it hogwash—most likely the creation of storyteller Edward Rowe Snow—but some believe the long-dead wife of a Confederate prisoner inhabits the island to this day.

A walk along the seawall and tidal pools are other pleasant ways to enjoy an afternoon. Just leave the starfish and other wildlife for future visitors to discover. You're welcome to toss a ball or a Frisbee or imagine yourself a soldier stationed here during WWII, passing the time with a game of baseball.

KID-FRIENDLY EATS: The best way to appreciate the splendor of George's Island is to dine alfresco, as picnics are welcome. If you left the cooler at home, you can grab simple eats (hot dogs, burgers, etc.) at the seasonal on-site **snack bar,** near the dock. There are also snack bars on board the boats that bring you here. Despite its name, the **Dockside Restaurant & Sports Bar** (183 State St., tel. 617/723–7050), outside Fanueil Hall, does have a children's menu.

Leave it to the folks at Harvard to find a way around the laws of physics. This group of natural history museums may look finite on the outside, but inside it seems to go on forever. (Too bad they haven't found a way around the parking nightmare; take public transportation instead.)

The natural history museum umbrella comprises three separate galleries: the Botanical Museum, the Museum of Comparative Zoology, and the Mineralogical and Geological Museum. This last one showcases Mother Nature's baubles in display-case-filled rooms that resemble the world's largest jewelry store. Here you can see rocks and minerals from ordinary quartz to birthstones and even learn how the gems got associated with specific months. More fascinating still is the meteor exhibit, featuring great slabs of space debris that have fallen to earth—some thousands of years old.

There's more ancient history in the Museum of Comparative Zoology. Dino-loving kids will have a field day exploring the jumbo prehistoric leftovers, including a plateosaurus from the

HEY, KIDS! If entomology (the study of insects) is your bag, you can't beat the ode to the beetles—the bugs, not the singers. Display cases in the zoology museum are filled with preserved specimens. Note to creepy crawly–phobes: Prepare yourself. Some of these guys are big and scary, even if they *are* dead. The Ghostwalker Beetle, for example, is about the size of a small rat. If eyeballing isn't enough, you can get a closer look with one of the tethered magnifying glasses.

Triassic period and an elephant-size mastodon from…New Jersey. Another highlight is the mind-boggling collection of taxidermic animals, which your kids will either love or hate depending on their stance on animal rights. For the record, these specimens—an impressive lot including tigers, bears, and whales—were collected more than a century ago, when people felt differently about such things. Regardless, the proximity you can get to some of these creatures is breathtaking. Suffice it to say that it'll be the closest you'll ever get (hopefully, anyway) to the mouth of a lion.

In between these two galleries is the botanical museum, which might seem ho-hum until you take a closer look. Display cases contain thousands of incredible flower reproductions, lifelike right down to the insects. Fashioned as educational tools between 1887 and 1936 (colorful textbooks didn't exist 100 years ago), the world-famous Glass Flowers collection of replicas, made by father and son Leopold and Rudolf Blaschka, is made entirely of glass; many people walk by a time or two before realizing they're fakes.

KEEP IN MIND:

The building housing the natural history museum also houses the Peabody Museum of Archaeology and Ethnology, containing cultural artifacts from around the world. Kids' reaction to this museum is usually less animated than to the zoology museum, however, so upon entering the building, turn left!

KID-FRIENDLY EATS: An old institution in Harvard Square, **Charlie's Kitchen** (10 Elliott St., tel. 617/492–9646) is known among locals for burgers—particularly double cheeseburgers. Around the corner from the museum, **Bertucci's** (21 Brattle St., tel. 617/864–4748) isn't as colorful, but it has dependable pizza and other Italian fare. Or try out the Mexican food at the **Border Cafe** (32 Church St., tel. 617/864–6100).

HIGGINS ARMORY MUSEUM

You'd expect to find a medieval castle in England—but in *New* England? Sure, it looks like an ordinary office building on the outside (except for the knight-in-shining-armor roof ornament), but inside is anything but ordinary. A reproduction of a 13th-century European castle, Higgins Armory is uncannily authentic, from its "stone" walls (really plaster) right down to its painstakingly applied faux age marks.

The late John Woodman Higgins built the palace in 1931 to house his enormous collection of armor. The ultimate fan of steel, the metal magnate traveled the world collecting, amassing an assortment that dates back to the days of the gladiators. In this stronghold, you'll encounter all the trappings of the Round Table denizens, not to mention the all-important coat of arms for their horses. All that's missing are the gallant knights themselves.

Suits of armor are spread over four floors. Plaques point out important details, such as how you can tell the difference between battle armor and jousting armor (the latter has a "target" plate over the left shoulder). On-site staff members are more than happy

KID-FRIENDLY EATS: Friendly, family-owned **Barbers Crossing** (325 W. Boylston St., tel. 508/852–3435) specializes in seafood, but the owners have thoughtfully included a children's menu with the all-important hot dogs, spaghetti, and the like. About a mile away is a **Friendly's** (451 Lincoln St., tel. 508/852–1470).

HEY, KIDS! Ever wonder what it was like to live in a medieval castle? Here's one rule: Children were not allowed to eat in the formal dining room until they had mastered proper table manners. That meant eating only with the thumb, pointer, and middle finger of your right hand (southpaws had their left hands bound so they wouldn't forget). Sound severe? Well, there were some good points, too. You never got yelled at for wiping your hands on the tablecloth; napkins hadn't been invented yet.

100 Barber Ave. (I-190 Exit 1),
Worcester

 508/853-6015

 $5.75 ages 17 and up,
$4.75 children 6-16

 T-Sa 10-4, Su 12-4

5 and up

to answer questions. You might wonder, for example, why some of the armor is so ornate. "It's clothing," explains one staffer. "In addition to being protected, knights wanted to look cool."

Though the ambience is fantasy-inspiring, the no-touch aspect can make the Higgins a snooze to some kids, especially those used to interactive exhibits. Fortunately, the Higgins has those, too. A second-floor discovery center features kid-size lord and lady apparel to wear, as well as a few helmets to try on (they are h-e-a-v-y). If you're squeamish about sharing headgear with the entire court, get the knight's-eye view by putting your kisser up to a face plate mounted inside a block. Other activities include period games and occasional craft projects.

KEEP IN MIND: Demonstrations—during which some audience members might be asked to try on some of the weighty duds—take place twice daily in the auditorium on weekends and during school vacations. Ask about an occasional multimedia show in the Great Hall that re-creates some of the sights and sounds of a joust. If one is not scheduled, the staff will occasionally run it upon request. As for equipping yourself: Leave the enormous backpacks at home. Pieces of Higgins's collection have walked off (figuratively speaking) over the years, and the armory has had to respond by prohibiting big bags.

IMAGINATION WORKS

You know all those imaginative play places with tea parties and dress up? Well, consider this the "dad" version. No doubt kids of both sexes will love it here, but the landscape (note the rock-climbing wall and the bulldozer) has "male parent" written all over it.

It was two dads, in fact, who conceived the idea for this spot after habitually coming up short on local places to take their own kids. A couple of years later, they hung out their shingle on this 11,000-square-foot emporium of things to play with, climb on, and create.

Play areas are spread amid a large, mostly open space and include wooden train sets, a "campsite," and a water play area. You won't get more than 100 feet in the door, however, before being stopped by Mt. Imagination, where a rock-climbing wall is fitted with hand- and footholds to help you ascend. A treadmill apparatus underneath keeps the "rock" moving down, so climbers can scale continuously without reaching the top—good for acrophobic parents who can't bear the idea of rescuing a stuck child from the top of a 10-foot wall.

KEEP IN MIND: Imagination Works is busy but not chaotic, one of those places you can let your kids play and actually catch up with adult friends. This is a particular bonus in winter. The moral of this story? If you like it, consider frequent-visitor discounts, particularly if you have preschool children. Craft activities (painting, collage, etc.) are offered in the art studio throughout the day, but ask about staff-member-led workshops that happen only at scheduled times.

Other adventure areas include a kid-size train (caboose, engine, and dining car) and a full-size (nonworking) steam shovel, with moveable levers in the cab. At the bubble cocoon, children stand on a platform and try to envelop themselves in a king-size soap bubble, but it's harder than it looks. And just try to get your kids away from the fully loaded, remote-control truck set.

Kids under 5 get their own picket-fence-rimmed Little Folks Farms, complete with apple tree, garden, gardening tools, and vegetable market. Beach babies will like the oversize sandbox with all the essentials—shovels, pails, and a sunny ocean scene. The best part? The place is sparkling clean, right down to the bathrooms.

HEY, KIDS! The glass wall at the center's entrance is screaming for your artwork. Grab a marker (ask for the special ones kept around just for this purpose) and go to town. You can even play tictacktoe. Just try doing that at home...then again, maybe not!

KID-FRIENDLY EATS: The on-site **IW Cafe** has all the staples: PB & Js, macaroni and cheese, chicken nuggets, and soups and such for grownups as well as plenty of snacks. Across the street, **T.G.I. Friday's** (1 Worcester Rd., Framingham, tel. 508/875-7735) has an extensive menu of sandwiches, salads, soups, ribs, and just about anything else you can think of.

JOHN F. KENNEDY LIBRARY AND MUSEUM

Let's face it. As hard (and depressing!) as it is to believe, the Kennedy administration registers as much like ancient history to today's children as the Roosevelt administration does to us parents. Yet nearly four decades after its untimely end, John F. Kennedy's brief term in the White House continues to read more like a fable than political history. True, some of the rosy details have shown a few thorns over the years, but the story of the handsome politician and his beautiful bride has lost little luster, remaining a captivating historical moment to be discovered at the Kennedy Library.

Start your visit with a 17-minute film that introduces you to the brash young senator, from the beginning of his meteoric rise right up to his 1960 nomination to the Democratic presidential ticket. The exhibits that follow represent a time line of the ensuing years, telling stories through props, film clips, front pages, and photos.

That Mr. Kennedy was the country's first media president is displayed vividly through numerous video snippets. The president held 63 press conferences during his short

KID-FRIENDLY EATS: At the cafeteria-style **Museum Cafe,** the food won't bowl you over, but the setting—overlooking the pavilion—is pleasant. **Phillips Old Colony House** (780 Morrissey Blvd., tel. 617/282–7700) is easy to reach and easy on your kids; it's got salads, sandwiches, steaks, and a nice-size children's menu.

HEY, KIDS! You'll learn all sorts of interesting things about Kennedy and about people here. For instance, JFK's charisma made him one of the country's most popular presidents, which might lead you to believe that he won the 1960 election by a landslide. In reality, the 43-year-old Kennedy (the youngest president ever elected) received only 118,550 votes (just .2% of those voting) more than future president Richard Nixon. By the middle of Kennedy's term in office, however, he was so popular that *well* more than half the country claimed to have voted for him.

Columbia Point (I–93 Exit 15)

 $8 adults, $4 children 13–17

 Daily 9–5

617/929–4500

10 and up

term in the White House, cementing his image in the public memory and revolutionizing the amount of access the nation had (and continues to have) to its highest public officer. Features of the tour—including some re-created areas of the White House, and handwritten notes and letters—provide fascinating glimpses into the era, educating in an amiable, accessible manner. Jacqueline admirers will find the former first lady well represented, too; look for some of her notes and photos, as well as a pillbox hat or two.

Don't miss a visit to the Situation Theater, where videos replay anxious moments from the Cuban Missile Crisis, when the threat of the atomic bomb loomed in our backyard. The footage provides a chilling reminder of the specter of nuclear war.

KEEP IN MIND: The library is best for schoolkids familiar with this period in history. If you're bringing younger students, pick up the "Treasures of the Kennedy Library" guide, outlining a scavenger hunt of sorts through the museum. Also make time to appreciate the stellar views of the city across the water. The dramatic glass pavilion atrium is a poignant tribute to Kennedy and a lovely place to watch the world go by. To get closer to the water, descend steps outside the building. From May to November, look for JFK's *Victura*, a sloop given to him when he was 15, docked outside.

JOHN HANCOCK OBSERVATORY

Sure, it pales by about 50 stories compared to such monoliths as New York City's World Trade Center. Nevertheless, the Hancock Tower, designed by renowned architect I.M. Pei, owns Boston's vertical superiority title, towering at least 10 stories over its next-tallest neighbor, the Prudential Center (*see below*).

The gleaming edifice was completed in 1976, a glittering contrast to the rather homely Pru. Not that this structure was without its troubles. Legend has it that shortly after construction, improper windows (a problem that has since been repaired) shed some glass on the streets below.

That building developers planned for their creation's prominence on the tourist trail becomes abundantly clear the moment you step off the 60-floor elevator. The souvenir stand is one clue, the coin-operated binoculars another. Nevertheless, all of that sparkling glass does make for some stunning views in three directions (the southern exposure is blocked by a function room).

KID-FRIENDLY EATS: There are no restaurants in the building, unfortunate during Boston's frigid winter. You can minimize the freeze (or heat) factor by walking a block to the Westin Hotel (10 Huntington Ave., tel. 617/262–9600), at Copley Square, where you'll find indoor blocks worth of restaurants. The **Au Bon Pain** (100 Huntington Ave., tel. 617/ 247–9467), right near the entrance, is unusually large and comfy, with counters full of tasty salads, sandwiches, soups, bagels, and baked goods. Another short walk outdoors brings you to **T.G.I. Friday's** (26 Exeter St., tel. 617/266–9040) and its enormous selection of sandwiches, salads, and entrées.

Like its shiny facade, the Hancock Tower offers spiffy shows and exhibits. Touch-screen computer kiosks are sprinkled along the banks of windows, offering everything from trivia challenges to panoramic city footage to step-by-step travel directions to your next destination. Numerous photographs detail the history of some of Boston's most famous landmarks and where to look for them. On the building's northeast side, you can look toward Logan Airport (3 miles away) while eavesdropping (via radio) on communications between the control tower and incoming pilots.

The drama of the American Revolution is re-created in a multimedia presentation that uses a relief map, lights, and sound effects. The 11-minute show, entitled "Road to Independence," adeptly encapsulates the major events of the war and details the painstaking efforts—and tons of landfill—it later took to expand the once-puny Boston. That explains why, in the early part of the show, a model of the Hancock Tower is sitting in the middle of water.

KEEP IN MIND:
Many people accidentally by-pass the downstairs ticket booth and head directly up the eleva-tor to the observation deck. Bad move. There are no ticket sales upstairs, and you'll be sent back down to pay admission.

HEY, KIDS! Impress your friends with your weather-predicting skills. The top of the Old John Hancock Tower, across the street on Berkley Street, flashes colors to indicate the day's climate. So, memorize the poem: "Steady blue, clear view; flashing blue, clouds are due; steady red, rain ahead; flashing red, snow instead, unless it's summer, when it means the Red Sox game has been postponed."

LASER QUEST

Boston is loaded with sights and attractions that can be called educational. This isn't one of them. Of course, that will probably delight many kids (and some parents) whose soul's desire is to spend an afternoon with a ray gun playing space ranger.

So why play here? Enthusiasts know Laser Quest as a preeminent, er, force in the field. While other emporiums peddle the attraction as a side note, Laser Quest is all lasers, all the time. There are a couple of video games and a Ping-Pong table in the lobby, but that's just to help you pass the time while you wait for your turn.

Play sessions are 15 minutes long—double the amount you'd play at most other places—and take place in a vast, 8,000-square-foot, multilevel arena. That may not sound huge, but it will feel gargantuan when you're standing in the dark surrounded by artificial fog.

KID-FRIENDLY EATS: Right in the parking lot, **Spud's Restaurant & Pub** (139 Endicott St., tel. 978/774–7786) serves good pub food. The name of the **Sylvan Street Grille** (12 Sylvan St., tel. 978/774–1724) makes the menu self-explanatory. Characters such as Barney sometimes show up on weekends.

KEEP IN MIND: There are no official rules on shoes or clothing. Veterans, however, counsel newcomers to avoid white or light clothing that will glow under the arena's lights. You can take that advice for whatever it's worth. As the general manager points out, "Everybody is wearing flashing lights, so it's not like you're going to be able to hide." Kids ages 5 and 6 can play, but they'll have to team up with an adult; the grown-up wears the vest, while the child totes the laser. In that case, both play for the price of one.

139 Endicott St. (Rte. 128 Exit 24), Danvers

 Late June–Labor Day, F–Sa 12–12, Su–Th 2–11; early Sept–late June, T–Th 4–9, F 4–12, Sa 10 AM–12 AM, Su 12–6

978/762-8778

 $6.50 per game

 7 and up

Up to 39 players take to the arena at once. Unlike team games, at Laser Quest it's every man, woman, and child for him- or herself. Your goal is to zap as much—and get zapped as little—as possible. Blinking lights on each player's vest serve as the targets. Players are supplied with unlimited shots, which means no lost time reloading mid-game, but be prepared for a little equipment down time (about five seconds) each time you're tagged. Scorecards at the end tally who tagged whom and how often and determine the winner. Grown-ups: Don't think you hold any advantage here. One of the best things about the game is the level playing field. There are no benefits to size, gender, or age. As one staff member put it, "It all depends on your aim." Besides, you should know by now that where high-tech gadgets are concerned, the kids have it all over us.

HEY, KIDS! Now's your chance to adopt an alias. For the duration of the game, Laser Quest players give up their given names in favor of whatever nickname they choose: Darth Vader, Geodude, Little Bo Peep, it doesn't matter. The name will show up on your scorecard and the score-cards of those you hit. There are a couple of essential no-no's, though. Names with violent, obscene, or religious implications are strictly prohibited.

LE GRAND DAVID & HIS OWN SPECTACULAR MAGIC COMPANY

Copperfield, Shmopperfield. Who needs *that* David when the North Shore town of Beverly gives you this one (dramatically pronounced Da–veed). True, you won't see vanishing jets or disappearing sphinxes, but what you do get is humor, fun, and a little bit of good old-fashioned prestidigitation. And from your seat in this intimate theater, you won't need high-power binoculars to see.

Nearly everything about this charming show is a throwback, from the glittery costumes to the handsome barbershop quartet. A dashing, tuxedoed usher welcomes you in, player-piano music tinkles in the lobby, and Harlequin-attired jugglers entertain as you await the rise of the curtain. The company itself—headed by elder statesman Marco the Magi (Cesareo Pelaez), not by David, who is also a leading player—thinks of its style as "classic." The theater is similarly well aged. Built in 1920 by a pair of vaudeville-era entertainers, the palace has been lovingly restored by the Grand David troop, who purchased it back in 1977.

KEEP IN MIND: Tickets for the show are often available the same day, as the Cabot Theater holds 700 seats. However, since there is no reserved seating, it's best to show up 30 minutes before the show starts as the best spots fill up early. If parking can't be found on the street, you can find spaces in a municipal lot around the corner. The company's other show, "An Anthology of Stage Magic," is also good for kids; it's performed on sporadic Saturdays, October–May, at the nearby Larcom Theater.

Perhaps the greatest piece of magic is how the troop maintains the scope of the show. A self-supporting company, the players construct their own props, dress their own stage, and sew their own costumes—the latter a particularly daunting task since dozens of players make myriad wardrobe changes in every performance. That isn't to say that the finished product looks homemade. True, there is a homespun quality to the extended-family troop's performance style, and there's a hint of the hokey along with the dramatic. But the illusions will leave you scratching your head, and performers and stagehands pull it all off with aplomb, a fact evidenced by the hundreds of spectators who visit each week.

Great fun as it is, do consider your child's age and disposition before buying tickets. At roughly 2¼ hours (with an intermission), the show may be too long for really little ones.

HEY, KIDS! To become a magical legend, you need more than stellar slight of hand. You need time. The Grand David company has been performing for over a quarter century, appearing in the *Guinness Book of World Records* as the "longest running resident stage magic production/show." Now that's magic!

KID-FRIENDLY EATS: The theater's old-style ambience is finished off with an upstairs **cafe** featuring yummy cookies and baked goods, just like homemade. That's not the best news for parents, since snacking during the late-afternoon show can do in an appetite for dinner. If you are hungry, the **Cabot Place Restaurant** (256 Cabot St., tel. 978/927–3920) has light (soups, salads) and heavier (seafood casseroles and Newburgs) fare as well as a children's menu. Homemade Italian favorites are on hand at **Cafe Salerno** (73 Cabot St., tel. 978/927–1979).

LIBERTY FLEET OF TALL SHIPS

Centuries after being dethroned as the most efficient form of transoceanic transportation, the tall ship has re-emerged as a beloved form of aquatic transit. And it's no wonder. These gallant ladies are a sight, drawing contented sighs as their billowing sails pass on the horizon and earning a place in the sailing public's heart.

Boston families without the wherewithal to actually own one of these esteemed ladies (or the gastrointestinal constitution to embark on a multiday ocean voyage) needn't remain mere spectators. Each spring, the Liberty Fleet's two sizeable schooners arrive in Boston from their winter port in Key West, Florida, and invite visitors aboard for an afternoon of tall-ship sailing splendor.

Prospective mateys can choose from two schooners: the 125-foot *Liberty Clipper* or the 80-foot *Liberty*. Both are accurate replicas of two-masted, 18th-century fishing vessels, the kind you would have seen tooling around the nation's coastlines more than 100 years ago.

KEEP IN MIND: Reservations for all sails are essential, as are plenty of sunscreen and a light sweater. Breezes on the open sea can chill passengers even on a sultry day.

KID-FRIENDLY EATS: Beverages are available for purchase on all sails. In addition to the regular daily schedule, the Liberty Fleet offers weekly brunch sails at 11 Sunday morning ($45 ages 13 and up, $25 children 12 and under). **Waves Bar and Grill** (Marriott Long Wharf, 296 State St., tel. 617/227–0800) features grills, burgers, pizzas, and lots of other choices. Indulge in Italian cuisine at **Lodo Restaurant & Café** (210 Hanover St., tel. 617/720–0052).

67 Long Wharf

617/742-0333

$30 ages 13 and up, $18 children 12 and under

Memorial Day–Sept, daily 12, 3, and 6

All ages

Daily voyages depart Long Wharf for 2½-hour scenic tours of Boston Harbor. Precisely where you'll go varies each day; this is a sailing ship, after all. "It all depends on which way the winds blows," declares a crew member. If you're not content to merely sit on the sidelines feeling the wind in your hair (although there's a lot to be said for this), you're welcome to pitch in as an honorary crew member and help hoist the sails, an onerous task that requires abundant hands on deck. Of course, the ship needs to be steered, too, and little ones are often invited to try their hand at the helm. And since this is a pleasure cruise, you needn't worry about being ordered to swab the deck.

HEY, KIDS! Experienced seafarers speak in a language all their own. "Charley Noble," for example, is not a "who" but rather a "what"; it's actually the galley stovepipe. (Remember this if someone ever sends you to go find "him.") "Avast," as in "Avast ye mateys," means "stop what you're doing." "Ahoy" is a call to attract attention, and "Aargh," is, well, self-explanatory.

MAKE WAY FOR DUCKLINGS TOUR

F olks outside New England may consider a certain quacker down in Orlando to be the world's most notable waterfowl. Among Bostonians, however, there are no ducks more famous than those in the Mallard family.

As most anyone over the age of 3 knows, the Mallards are the title characters in Robert McCloskey's famed children's book *Make Way for Ducklings*. On the hunt for a home, Mrs. Mallard and her clan of eight—Jack, Kack, Lack, Mack, Nack, Ouack, Pack, and Quack—hold up traffic as they endeavor to cross a busy Boston street. (Those who've been pedestrians in this city can attest that there is no higher drama than that.)

Walking in the Mallards' web prints begins at the visitor center on the Boston Common. Travelers first get a quick refresher course on the story and then a bit of history of the Common. Most sights on the 1½-hour trip (reservations required) appear just the way they did in McCloskey's drawings. These include the State House on Beacon Hill, Louisburg Square, and the building that was the Old Corner Bookstore. Though it's now a 7-11, most kids

KEEP IN MIND: Though tour guides carry a copy of the book, they don't often read from it along the way, so it's not a bad idea to bring a copy for your own reference. Each Mother's Day, Historic Neighborhoods celebrates the story with Make Way for Ducklings Day. Tourists, many dressed up as their favorite character, gather on the Common and proceed to parade (no tour this day) through Beacon Hill back to the Public Garden, where there is entertainment and snacks. Tickets are $10 in advance for a family of four.

can easily recognize it from its unique design. (Tour guides are experts in city architecture and lore and ably build in a bit of age-appropriate history, encouraging kids to recognize different designs in Boston's landmarks.) The tour winds down at the Public Garden, which you'll enter, just as Mrs. Mallard did, through the gate on the corner of Beacon Street. Bronze casts of some of the Mallard clan provide a fitting final stop.

Historic Neighborhoods, the nonprofit group that runs the tour, does its best to remain true to the story, but certain liberties are taken. Mr. and Mrs. Mallard actually flew *over* the Beacon Hill State House. For obvious reasons, however, you'll have to be content to walk through.

KID-FRIENDLY EATS: To-die-for flat bread and yummy fillings (caramelized onions, etc.) at **Cosi Sandwich Bar** (53 State St., tel. 617/723–3369) will please adults but might raise eyebrows among kids. The **Silvertone Bar & Grille** (69 Bromfield St., tel. 617/338–7887) has a funky, retro style.

HEY, KIDS! How did Robert McCloskey draw so accurately? The author was once a budding artist attending classes at Vesper George Art School, right in Boston. During his apprentice days, McCloskey made drawings while gazing out the window of his apartment near Louisburg Square. Who said daydreaming is a waste of time? Be sure to ask about McCloskey's apartment on the tour.

MINUTE MAN NATIONAL HISTORICAL PARK

S ome history you read about; some you see. At Minute Man National Historical Park, history is something you can practically feel.

It may sound hokey, but the rustic stretches of battlefield here nearly echo with long-ago events. Several hundred years ago—April 19, 1775, to be precise—British and Colonial soldiers clashed for the first time, firing that infamous "shot heard round the world."

The park comprises more than 900 acres. Begin at the new Minuteman Visitor Center, in Lexington, where a new multimedia presentation—"Road to Revolution"—orients you to what's ahead. Next, access the Battle Road Trail right outside the visitor center. This 5½-mile stretch is the park's longest continuous section of off-road path, wending through fields traveled by the 18th-century soldiers. Wind up your trek at Meriam's Corner, in Concord. Along the way, look for historic buildings, such as the Hartwell Tavern (open mid-May to October, with costumed interpreters but no grub and ale!), broken cobblestone walls, and crumbled foundations, as well as markers spelling out events.

HEY, KIDS!

The first shot of the American Revolution was fired early on April 19 on the Lexington Green. Eight colonists died. Ralph Waldo Emerson's "shot heard round the world" was actually fired later at the North Bridge, which was where the first British soldiers fell.

KEEP IN MIND: Crowds jam the trails on summer weekends, so to appreciate the solemnity of the place, come on an off-season weekday. Look for parking signs on major roads, and pick up trail maps at either of the visitor centers. Reenactments are held each Patriots Day weekend, and other events are held throughout the year (call 978/369–6993 for a schedule). Two good spots to learn more about local and American history are the Concord Museum (200 Lexington Rd., Concord, tel. 978/369–9609) and the Museum of Our National Heritage (33 Marrett Rd., Lexington, tel. 781/861–6559).

North Bridge Visitor Center,
174 Liberty St., Concord

978/369–6993 or
781/862–7753

Visitor centers free; some
historic sites charge

Daily sunrise–sunset; visitor centers
May–Oct, daily 9–5; Nov–Apr, daily 9–4

All ages

A separate, shorter (.4-mile), but equally stirring trail leads to the North Bridge. The small span was once a confrontation point for British and Colonial soldiers. The perils seem palpable when you realize just how close these armed adversaries stood to one another. You'll also find the Minute Man Statue here as well as the North Bridge Visitor Center.

You don't have to be a history lover to enjoy the park. Since most paths are far removed from the road (though there are a couple of crosswalks), some people come here just for its good hiking and biking. On the other hand, virtually everyone would appreciate the "Road to Revolution," and the fact that trails are intertwined with history is certainly an added bonus. To get the kids into it, ask at one of the visitor centers about the Junior Ranger Activity Booklet ($1.50).

KID-FRIENDLY EATS: After a long day of biking and hiking, you can get your fill of Italian favorites at **Bertucci's** (1777 Massachusetts Ave., Lexington, tel. 781/860–9000). Other options include the **Country Kitchen** (181 Sudbury Rd., Concord, tel. 978/371–0181) and additional suggestions under Walden Pond.

MUSEUM OF FINE ARTS

Who says art appreciation is just about looking? While the preeminent image of the art world may be of echoing corridors and sacrosanct vestibules, more and more museums—like this one—are getting away from the whole "hallowed halls" thing. Says one MFA staff member, "It's hard to consider our halls hallowed when we've got kids running around with glue and ink in their hands."

Such art supplies are available in abundance through the MFA's Family Place, which offers weekend workshops (during the school year) that equip kids with materials to help them experiment with art as well as appreciate it. Brightly colored packets distributed through the program are themed for a particular type of art. (The Asian packet, for example, includes rice paper.) Walk among the art, and then try your hand in the downstairs workshop. Pamphlets guide you to the appropriate gallery and even suggest follow-up reading materials. Themes change each weekend, and materials change with each theme. Elaborate activities continue daily during school vacation weeks; a Hats and Headdresses project, for example, ran in conjunction with an exhibit of tiaras.

KEEP IN MIND: Family Place is held October to June, Saturday and Sunday from 11 to 4. School vacation week activities take place Monday through Friday from 10 to 4 during February and April breaks. Children's Room programs are held 3:30 to 4:45, Monday to Friday (September to June) and Monday to Thursday (July to August). To participate in any of these drop-in programs, check in at the front desk at the West Wing entrance on arrival.

465 Huntington Ave.

 617/267-9200

$12 adults, $5 children
7–17 school days until 3,
free other times

 M–T 10–4:45, W–F 10–9:45 (Th–F after 5
West Wing only), Sa–Su 10–5:45

4 and up

Of course, you can make forays on your own any day. The MFA's "Paper Guides," two-page pamphlets that detail a particular exhibit and proffer scavenger-hunt-type explorations, are always available. And kids who'd truly like to explore the museum on their own—in other words, without you—can do so at the Children's Room. The free, after-school drop-off program (for children 6–12) features supervised museum exploration and art workshops.

To make budding art lovers less reluctant, experts counsel parents to focus on one gallery (a good idea since this museum is B-I-G) and to avoid weekend crowds, if possible. Also check out the museum shop's collection of kids' books. Though you'll have to navigate around some typical souvenir-y items (accordion anyone?), there are some exceptional kid-oriented art books that are worth a look.

HEY, KIDS! Try your hand at the masters. The MFA encourages you to bring pencils and pads and to try and sketch some of these magnificent pieces of art.

KID-FRIENDLY EATS: There are four restaurants at the museum. The most appropriate—i.e., the one with hot dogs and sandwiches—is the **Court-yard Café.** Off property, continue the adventure with Thai food at the **Brown Sugar Cafe** (129 Jersey St., tel. 617/266–2928). If it's grill fare you're after, try **Thorntons Fenway Grill** (100 Peterborough St., tel. 617/421–0104).

MUSEUM OF SCIENCE

Think of this spiffy institution in the eponymously named Science Park as an arcade for your brain. There are gadgets and gizmos aplenty, but each is designed to teach you something more than how to maximize your Super Mario score.

The museum claims roots back more than a century and a half, but this is no dinosaur. Interactive exhibits here—and there are more than 600 of them—are state-of-the-art, and you don't need to be a mini Albert Einstein to appreciate them. Novel concepts engage even the science-phobe.

Three floors offer a dizzying number of exhibits—too many to take in on one visit. Swings and seesaws provide the structure for learning about fulcrums and gravity in Science in the Park. Optical illusions will bowl you over in Seeing is Deceiving. Kids can spend hours bounding up and down the musical stairs in the Red Wing atrium. The 20-foot model of a Tyrannosaurus Rex is a time-honored kid-favorite, and the addition of the 3-D Virtual Fish Tank, a virtual undersea spot in which you can create computer-generated fish—

KID-FRIENDLY EATS: There's a whole universe of food available at the on-site **Galaxy Cafés,** which include the Starlite Deli, Pizza Gusta, and Galileo's. At the Cambridgeside Galleria, **Houlihan's** (100 Cambridgeside Pl., Cambridge, tel. 617/577–1660) serves burgers, sandwiches, salads, and kids' fare.

HEY, KIDS! Don't wait for a thunderstorm to appreciate the power of lightning. Presentations at the Theater of Electricity get you remarkably close to this striking phenomenon of nature—a much safer approach than Ben Franklin's kite-and-key method. Watch a human guinea pig escape peril when the cage he's in is repeatedly struck by bolts of electricity. How does he survive? Electricity will always follow the path of least resistance, which in this case is through the metal. Other demonstrations (safely) involve the audience. However, loud sounds and bright lights are not for the faint of heart.

Science Park, I-93 and Storrow Dr.

 $10 ages 12 and up, $7 children 3-11

 F 9-9, Sa-Th 9-5

 617/723-2500

 3 and up

and then instruct them to eat your friends' fish—marks the recent merger of the Museum of Science with the Computer Museum.

No visit to the museum is complete without a visit to either (or both!) the Mugar Omni Theater, which shows IMAX films, or the Charles Hayden Planetarium. Hour-long shows at the planetarium include "The Sky Tonight," detailing what to look for outside your door, and evening laser shows that many kids rate as awesome. Beautiful presentations and exceptionally entertaining hosts make the planetarium one of the museum's best spots and a good first stop any time you come.

Toddlers who can't appreciate the big-kid stuff can get a science primer at the Discovery Center. The 3,200-square-foot space has irresistible artifacts, such as an 18-foot python's skeleton, not to mention tons of experiments. Kids under 5 can try their hand at some water activities. There's even a soft-play corner for the smallest children.

KEEP IN MIND: The Museum of Science is big—really big. Biting off too much in one visit will probably leave you overwhelmed and under-satisfied. Live presentations (such as the "Live Animal Show" and "Lightning") take place daily, so make sure to check the schedule when you arrive. If you're planning to see an IMAX show, it's a good idea to call and order your tickets in advance, particularly on weekends. If you're into astronomy, be sure to ask about Friday Night Stargazing, when the museum opens its observatory to the public, weather permitting (reservations recommended).

One of the world's earliest automobiles has a very sophisticated-sounding French name: the Charron-Giradot et Voigt. The nickname is much more pedestrian: the toilet car. Perhaps the predecessor to today's lanky recreational vehicles, this 1906 oddster came equipped with a fold-out bed, a sink, and a working commode underneath one of the jump seats. Just call it the antidote to stop-and-go traffic.

This rare automobile (there were only a handful made) is one of the more noteworthy vehicles in residence at the Museum of Transportation, a place that's sure to be a hit with any kid who lights up when a classic automobile goes by. Dozens of colorful antiques (think *Chitty Chitty Bang Bang*) make up the collection, many dating back to the turn of the last century. With most of these horseless carriages, you'll have to settle for just looking, though you can climb on the occasional exhibit.

Two floors include numerous shiny old girls, and displays are rotated regularly. On any given day, you might come upon a 1908 Bailey Electric, a 1903 Gardner-Serpollet, or a

KEEP IN MIND: Before or after the museum, be sure to enjoy the rest of Larz Anderson Park, which includes a playground and romantic remnants of the old Anderson buildings, as well as some stellar views of Boston from the top of the hill. Weekends in summer, the museum hosts outdoor lawn events with food and activities. You won't want to miss the annual Brass and Gas Day (typically in June, call for exact date), when owners of pre-1916 cars take visitors for a ride.

15 Newton St., Brookline

617/522-6547

 $5 ages 17 and up,
$3 children 6–16

 T–Su 10–5

 All ages

1901 Winton racing car. The interactive exhibit Kids on the Move heralds child-powered locomotion, including bikes (such as Boneshakers, those big-wheeled tricycles) and skates. A small activity center features a wooden climb-on car representing the back end of a trolley, with working bell and crafts.

The museum sits on the grounds of the larger Larz Anderson Park. Anderson and his wife, Isabelle, owned many of the cars on display here and once used the sprawling 64-acre property (which Isabelle willed to the town of Brookline upon her death in 1948) as a summer estate. The museum building was built to store the estate's original vehicles: horses and carriages. It's amazing to think that this castlelike structure—many times bigger than most palatial residences—was really just a glorified garage with servants' quarters.

HEY, KIDS! Before the automobile, travelers relied on the good graces of equine transportation. Just like today's cars, these spiffy beauties required fuel—in the form of hay—and gave off toxic emissions—namely 20 pounds of manure each day.

KID-FRIENDLY EATS: In the park, there are some lovely pond-side areas that make for good picnicking grounds. **Legal Sea Foods** (43 Boylston St. [Rte. 9], Chestnut Hill, tel. 617/277–7300) offers plenty of choices from the sea. For tasty Italian specialties, try **Papa Razzi** (199 Boylston St., Chestnut Hill, tel. 617/527–6600).

NEW ENGLAND AQUARIUM

There are lots of good reasons to visit Boston's Central Wharf. Myrtle is one of the best: At 500 pounds, she's a sizeable lady—green head, thick shell, and all.

Myrtle, of course, is a sea turtle, a senior resident of the 30+-year-old New England Aquarium. Though she ranks as one of the most popular (and certainly one of the biggest) of the lot, she's in good company. She swims alongside more than 800 other sea creatures in the 200,000-gallon, four-story Ocean Tank that dominates the indoor landscape. You can view the action from virtually any angle, thanks to numerous windows and a ramp that spirals around the tank. It's simply hogfish heaven.

The rest of the aquarium features scads of denizens of the sea. Penguins cavort in the open-air rookery on the first floor. Seals engage visitors from their tank out front, while sea otters entertain guests out back. The third-floor Edge of the Water area lets you handle a few creatures, including starfish and horseshoe crabs. Interactive exhibits throughout teach about the ecology and conservation of the harbor, shore, and reef.

KID-FRIENDLY EATS: The on-site **Harbor View Café** features an adequate selection of burgers, hot dogs, sandwiches, and snacks. It may seem almost cannibalistic, but **Legal Sea Foods** (255 State St., tel. 617/742-5300) does have some of the best catches (broiled, fried, or baked) in town.

KEEP IN MIND: Crowds make the dark, narrow confines of the aquarium tough to navigate. Good visiting times are Sunday before noon and after 1 during the week. (Avoid Saturday completely if you can.) Not only will you steer clear of crowds, but you'll cut your wait time to get in. Admissions lines here are notoriously long, a particularly unwelcome circumstance in winter, since ticket booths are outside. Become a member, and skip the line completely. The new and as yet uncrowded Exploration Center features interactive exhibits and an activity center—a quiet place to get away from it all.

Central Wharf

 617/973-5200

Off-peak $12.50 ages 12 and up, $6.50 children 3–11; July–Labor Day, Sa–Su $14.50 ages 12 and up, $8 children

July–Labor Day, M, T, F 9–6, W–Th 9–8, Sa–Su 9–7; early Sept–June, M–F 9–5, Sa–Su 9–6

All ages

Go with the Flow, on the other hand, takes you into a totally different ecosystem: sewers. The interactive What Happens When You Flush feature is a real kid-pleaser, particularly when they activate the computer-generated "whoosh."

Yet another don't-miss highlight is Tyler. The loveable, irresistible 700-pound sea lion is the star of his own show on the permanently docked ship *Discovery*. He swims, slides, and even graces a lucky few with a fish-breath kiss. Like all other features here, the show is designed to educate, in this case demonstrating how human actions can be detrimental to nature. The lessons are well done, but Tyler is also simply a hoot to watch. The facility also offers whale watches and other aquatic nature explorations.

HEY, KIDS! How many different penguins can you identify? The penguin rookery has three types: African (classic black and white), rockhoppers (look for funny-looking yellow feathers on their heads), and little blues (tiny guys weighing no more than 2 pounds). Incidentally, the African variety is nicknamed the "jackass penguin" because of the braying sound it makes.

NEW ENGLAND SPORTS MUSEUM

W hen this interactive sports museum moved from its old digs in the Cambridgeside Galleria to its current home at the FleetCenter, the parking situation became dicier (hint: use the North Station garage). But the benefits of the new place far outweigh the disadvantages.

Perched on the fifth floor of the shiny new sports arena (the one that replaced the Boston Garden in body, if not in local sports enthusiasts' hearts), this rehabbed facility is a fan's dream. Though actual exhibit space numbers only about 10,000 square feet, the arena-side location, from which you can actually eyeball the Bruins' frozen rink and the Celtics' famous parquet floor, makes it seem much more impressive. Come early on a game day (around 10:30), and you may even spot the home teams and visitors conducting their practice shoot- or skate-arounds (no guarantees, though).

Exhibits and memorabilia are spread over two levels. Look for displays on hockey, basketball, baseball, and the Boston Marathon, to name a few. Those who haven't gotten over the

KID-FRIENDLY EATS: In addition to having great food, the **Fours** (166 Canal St., tel. 617/720– 4455) has nearly enough memorabilia to be considered a sports museum itself. At the **Commonwealth Fish & Beer** (138 Portland St., tel. 617/523–8383), you can enjoy pub fare while gazing at enormous brew tanks. And don't forget the North End, with all its incredible Italian restaurants and pastry shops.

1 FleetCenter

617/624-1234 recording,
617/787-7678 voice

$5 ages 12 and up, $4
children 11 and under

 T-Sa 10-5, Su 12-5

 10 and up

demise of the Garden can wax nostalgic in actual Boston Garden seats while watching
a video on the grande dame, or imagine themselves sitting out a call for high sticking
in a genuine Bruins penalty box. There's plenty more nostalgia at the ESPN kiosk,
where you can call up footage of the 100 greatest sports moments. Two highlights:
the 1980 U.S. Olympic hockey victory and hometown hero Doug Flutie's Hail Mary
pass in the Cotton Bowl.

There are a few interactive games as well. The mitts-down favorite is the Roger
Clemens catch. In this virtual game, you catch a strikeout and actually feel
the "thump" of the ball as it "falls" into your mitt. The Rocket also dispenses
a few tidbits about his form (spitting not included). While you're here, look
for computer hookups to various Internet sports sites.

KEEP IN MIND:
Because of its location, the museum occasionally closes down—during sound checks on the day of a concert, for example. Call ahead to be sure it's open. As parking is often a nightmare, opt for public transportation (the Green Line's North Station) when you can.

HEY, KIDS! Zambonis weren't always so easy to use. Before they became
motorized in the 1930s, ice groomers took the form of horse-drawn scrapers followed by attendants who spread hot water over the ice. (The hot water would fill
the cracks and freeze in a smoother sheet.) Because the process was so cumbersome, it was only done once per hockey game (as opposed to twice, as it is
today). And in case you're wondering, the horses did not wear skates.

OLD NORTH CHURCH

L isten my children and you shall hear... of the poetic license of Henry Wadsworth Longfellow. It seems the famous poet, author of "Paul Revere's Ride," took a few liberties in his work. There were at least two other riders on that famous night—William Dawes and Samuel Prescott—but how many good rhymes are there for those names? As for "two if by sea," the sea was actually the Charles River, not the Atlantic Ocean, but "the river" would have thrown off the meter completely.

Still, the poem's "North Church tower"—the one where "a lantern aloft in the belfry arch" was hung—is authentic and still standing. Nearly 300 years old, the city's oldest church still houses an active Episcopalian congregation (it was built in 1723 as a Church of England) and is open daily for tours (self-guided in the off-season).

Inside, you'll be struck by the chapel's novel setup. The stately house of worship proffered Boston's first premium "box seats" (long before the FleetCenter) in the form of pew boxes owned and occupied by wealthy merchant families. Pew fees paid for

KID-FRIENDLY EATS: The North End has some of the best Italian food around. Large portions and good prices at **La Famiglia** (112 Salem St., tel. 617/367–6711) have made it a family favorite. There's plenty more good Italian cooking at **Monica's** (148 Richmond St., tel. 617/720–5472).

KEEP IN MIND: Both the Behind the Scenes tours and the nighttime shows are offered only from June to October. Shows are given Thursday and Friday at 8, while tours are offered on the hour, weekdays between 10 and 5, weekends 1 to 5. The church suspends sightseeing for Sunday services at 9 and 11; however, the public is welcome to attend. Listen for the hour-long peal of the church bells every Sunday at noon. To get more information about Paul Revere, stop by the famous patriot's house (19 North Sq., tel. 617/523–1676).

the church's upkeep, and the boxes' high walls kept parishioners sheltered from the cold sea breezes. Plaques outside the doors note the names of original owners.

Guests are welcome year-round, but the best time to visit is in summer, when the Behind the Scenes program is running. It's then that tour guides lead you down to the church crypts, where more than 1,000 people—mostly original church members—are interred. Then travel two flights up to the bell tower, where those famous lanterns were hung. Though the church is a decidedly low-tech attraction, kids familiar with this period of history will get into the historical significance, particularly when they realize they're walking the same steps traveled in 1775 by Robert Newman, the church sexton who signaled Paul Revere. Mr. Revere himself also appears in summer, in a family-friendly one-hour nighttime show.

HEY, KIDS! Bells in the Old North Church are still rung by hand. While you listen, remember that this is the oldest peal in North America. For an extra treat, you can actually go up and watch them ring them bells on Sunday from 12 to 1. Better yet, ask mom and dad to go for rehearsal on Saturday. If you ask, the bell ringers might let you try your hand at it.

OLD STATE HOUSE MUSEUM

What's a Boston landmark doing in Chicago? That's the question tourists would have been asking had the Windy City gotten its way and relocated the Old State House to the banks of Lake Michigan.

The building's brush with the Midwest is but one piece of its lore. First home to the state's government offices, the building was a focal point during pre-Revolutionary War days. Numerous anti-British rallies met here, the Boston Massacre seethed just outside (look for a circle of commemorative cobblestones in the middle of the street in front of the building), and local leaders read the Declaration of Independence, two weeks after its signing, from the second-floor balcony.

Government ranks outgrew the site and moved to the current State House, on Beacon Hill, in 1798. Temporarily deemed obsolete (explaining why it was nearly shipped off to Chicago), the building was snatched up in 1881 by the Bostonian Society, which maintains it today as a landmark and museum (though it's owned by the city).

KID-FRIENDLY EATS: For something completely different, hike over to **Jacob Wirth** (31 Stuart St., tel. 617/338–8586), serving German specialties as well as traditional kid food. At Fanueil Hall, the **Salty Dog** (206 Fanueil Hall Marketplace, tel. 617/742–2094) has particularly good burgers and pub fare.

206 Washington St.

 617/720-1713

 $3 adults, $1 children 6–18, free for Massachusetts schoolchildren

 Daily 9-5

8 and up

Detailed inside are tidbits about the evolution of the building and the city around it, and audio dramatizations recount significant events. Revolutionary relics include John Hancock's coat (check out those fancy duds!) and tea from the Boston Tea Party (donated by the family of tea-party participant Thomas Melvill, who found some leftover tea in his boot). Revolutionary War aside, one of the most fascinating displays tells of Boston's development, from a roughly square-mile peninsula, whose only mainland access was a narrow road, to a thriving metropolis that was exponentially enlarged with trainloads of fill. Upstairs in the Council Chamber, look for more artifacts from the Revolutionary War: muskets, bullet molds, and uniform accessories, to name a few. This is also where you can see (but not go out on) the balcony from which the Declaration was read. Rotating interactive exhibits tend to address more modern events, such as Boston after World War II. For kids, ask at the front desk for a handout that lets them explore the museum via a scavenger hunt.

HEY, KIDS! History's a great thing, but so is the subway meter. A red light shoots up each time a T (the Blue and Orange lines, if you're interested) rumbles below. Officially, the light is there to record the stress level on this historic structure. Between you and me, though, it's just really cool.

KEEP IN MIND: Visiting this stately structure will take about 40 minutes to an hour, with the most captivated audience being kids studying the period in history. Though John Hancock's groovy duds may momentarily impress some little ones (grade 1 or lower), most of the historic value will be lost on them. On March 5 each year, the anniversary of the Boston Massacre is commemorated with a reenactment. Call for details.

OLD STURBRIDGE VILLAGE

Long before frozen pizzas and personal CD players, families lived in communities such as Old Sturbridge. Spread over 200 acres, this enormous living-history museum offers a glimpse into the life of a 19th-century village.

Opened in 1946, the museum is the result of painstaking effort. Designers scoured New England to create a perfect hamlet, whose 40 buildings, transported from throughout the area, include stores, tradespeople's shops, a parsonage, a district school, and a number of elegant residences. All have been lovingly restored inside and out. The finished product is surreal in its picture-perfection, from the pristine steeple of the Meetinghouse to the white picket fence of the Fitch House.

Costumed interpreters further the old-fashioned effect. In their straw bonnets and stovepipe hats, a village's worth of residents go about their business, plowing fields, husking corn, and tending to their daily chores. Like the buildings, characters have roots in actual history. For example, at Asa Knight's shop—an 1830s institution

HEY, KIDS!

Think your classroom is small? If you went to school 100 years ago, you would have shared a one-room schoolhouse with students of all ages. Check out the re-created version here, as well as other hands-on activities, at the Samson's Children's Museum.

KEEP IN MIND: You'll be walking a lot, mostly on dirt roads, so wear sturdy, comfortable shoes. There's probably too much to take in on one visit. If indeed you don't manage to see it all, you can obtain passes that allow you to return the next day. Of course, that will mean you'll either have to drive back and forth or spend the night at a local hostelry. Two options that continue the historical adventure are the Old Sturbridge Village Lodges and the Oliver Wight House (U.S. 20, tel. 508/347–3327), both owned by the village.

1 Old Sturbridge Village Rd.
(I-90 Exit 9), Sturbridge

 $18 ages 16 and up,
$9 children 6–15

 Jan–Washington's Birthday, Sa–Su 10–4; late Feb–
Mar and Nov–Dec, daily 10–4; Apr–Oct, daily 9–5

800/733-1830

 All ages

transplanted from Vermont—you may well find Asa himself behind the counter. Interpreters play their parts with aplomb, but there are some welcome limits: Old Sturbridge Village mercifully allows its 19th-century characters to answer questions in 21st-century English.

In addition to ambling among the day-to-day activities—a treat in and of itself—you can take part in special events. Among the village's hallmarks are Family Fun Days, held throughout the year: Storytelling, sleigh rides, and candle-making are offered during winter school vacation, music and outdoor games in summer. Listen for fife and drums during the Independence Day observance, or get in on a traditional 1830s Thanksgiving. During the fall harvest, you can even get your hands dirty, helping to dig potatoes, shell beans, and husk corn. All that hard manual labor may just make you and your kids appreciate those frozen pizzas back home.

KID-FRIENDLY EATS: At the village's **Bullard Tavern,** you can choose from a traditional midday buffet upstairs (with baked hams, meat pies, and such) or standard cafeteria fare (sandwiches and quiche) as well as some of the buffet offerings downstairs. Outside the village, the nearby **Picadilly Pub Restaurant** (362 Main St., tel. 508/347–8189) is a family favorite for chicken, fish, pastas, burgers, and probably just about anything else you can name.

OLD TOWN TROLLEY

Nothing screams "tourist" like a bevy of sightseers taking pictures out the window of a faux trolley car. Nevertheless, it's a shame that the folks who take advantage of this cute, albeit a little hokey, adventure are mostly out-of-towners. Tooling around in these green, old-fashioned "trolleys" (buses, actually) is a kick for kids, not to mention a great education for anybody who wants to learn about Boston. Even better, the trip accommodates restless young ones by allowing you to hop on and off to visit attractions along the way (except, of course, for the last tour of the day).

The 100-minute tours cover much of Boston and a little bit of Cambridge. Vehicles take you to all the important landmarks—the historic Freedom Trail, Copley Square, and Fanueil Hall, among them—and within a short T ride of others. Narration combines a little fact, a little legend, and a little lore, including such tidbits as which block is the city's most expensive (Louisburg Square) and what city garage was once condemned (Government Center's). You'll even get the lowdown on one of Boston's most popular nuptial spots; Trinity Church, the story goes, has a wait list that goes on for years, prompting hopeful young

KEEP IN MIND: Local experts (i.e., hotel doormen) consider Old Town to have the best narration of the trolley tours. The only catch to its on-again/off-again policy is that you are only allowed one complete circuit. If you'd like to ride around once and then make visits on a second go-round, take the red Beantown Trolley (tel. 617/236–2148), which allows you unlimited circuits. CityView (tel. 617/363–7899) advertises the city's only "multimedia enhanced" trolley tour. The best place to compare maps is near the aquarium, where all these operators have kiosks.

women to sign on before they've nabbed (or even met!) the groom. It's called "eternal optimism," according to the tour. As you can see, congenial narrator/drivers can't help but have fun, and dialogue is heavy on shtick. A sound track includes the theme song from *Cheers* as you pass the Bull Finch Pub and Ethel Merman singing about you-know-what business as you pass the theater district. It's all in good fun. Even the most cantankerous will have to work hard to keep from cracking a smile.

Technically, the circuit begins at the New England Aquarium (*see above*), but you can board at any of the trolley's 16 stops. Don't have a ticket? No problem. Drivers will let you ride now and pay later at the first stop with a ticket booth. The company also offers a nighttime Ghosts and Goblins Tour and an abbreviated Minuteman Tour.

KID-FRIENDLY EATS: Near the Northern Avenue Bridge, seafood-loving families can try the **Boston Sail Loft** (80 Atlantic Ave., tel. 617/227–7280) for tasty, dependable, and inexpensive food. The **Harp** (85 Causeway St., tel. 617/742–1010) serves traditional favorites (fish-and-chips, burgers) with Irish flair. Also see restaurant suggestions for the Prudential Center Skywalk and many other Boston sights—wherever you happen to be around lunchtime.

PIRATE ADVENTURE

Ah, the wonderful life of a pirate—the sailing, the salt air, the treasure, the robbing, pillaging, and plundering. Don't worry; it's only the first three you'll find on this fanciful adventure. A one-hour quest for pirate treasure on the open seas, this escapade provides about the best fantasy you'll find outside of Neverland.

The odyssey comes from the imagination of owner Than Drake, the self-proclaimed Captain Crisis, who built two ships (a second one launches from Orleans) expressly for the purpose of pirate play. Venturers from Hyannis cruise in the authentic-looking *Sea Gypsy*, a seemingly antique craft that is every bit the scalawag vessel, from the towering sail masts (they're a ruse—the ship is really a motorboat) to the cannons mounted on either side. Pirates-in-training get in the mood with a little facial decor, perhaps a painted-on eye patch or a twirly mustache. Everyone leaves his or her John Hancock (or Jean Laffitte) on the requisite pirate flag and gives a hand hoisting it into position. Then it's anchors aweigh.

HEY, KIDS!

Pretend pirates aren't the only ones who sailed these New England waters. Some very real scoundrels came through here as well. A few of the most notorious include William Kidd, Long John Avery, and the infamous Blackbeard. But don't worry! They're long gone.

KID-FRIENDLY EATS: The **Black Cat** (165 Ocean St., tel. 508/778–1233) seems a fitting place to dine after your pirate excursion. The tasty food is no pirate grub, though; it includes American grills and other specialties as well as a children's menu. Kids can feed themselves silly at the **Old Country Buffet** (1070 Iyanough Rd., tel. 508/790–1745), where the enormous daily chow table features such items as pizza and macaroni as well as chicken, mashed potatoes, and gravy.

Ocean St. Dock, Slip 3, Hyannis

 508/430-0202

$16 ages 3 and up, $8 children 2 and under

 Late June–Labor Day, M–Sa 9:30, 11, 12:30, 2, 3:30, and 5; Su 9:30, 11, and 12:30

3–10

Crew members plot the course based upon the "centuries-old" treasure map found on deck. To find the booty, you'll all have to keep a close eye out for clues—perhaps a floating bottle containing a message. There's peril as well; notorious scoundrel Pirate Pete appears bent on snagging the treasure for his very own. The threat is easily deflected with a blast from the super-powered cannons (ammunition: water). At last, "X" marks the spot of the treasure, and everyone lends a hand to haul it on board. There's no telling what you'll find—maybe doubloons. The festive trip home includes music and dancing and even a couple of rounds of the limbo. Once back at port, everyone gets a handful of booty to take home.

The *Sea Gypsy*'s small pirate crew—a captain and one other—runs the show from start to finish, interacting with little mateys all the way through. Parents can either join in or sit back and simply enjoy the ride.

KEEP IN MIND: It's never too early to make a reservation (people start calling for July 4 bookings on April 1, the day the phone lines open). Boats will not travel in strong winds or thunderstorms but will voyage as scheduled in light rain. Cool breezes can bring a chill on a hot day, so bring a sweater. While you're in town, enjoy some of Hyannis's other pleasures, including the Cape Cod Potato Chip Factory Tour (100 Breed's Hill Rd., tel. 508/775-7253) or some time on a beach. The Orleans boat docks behind the Goose Hummock sports shop.

PLASTER FUN TIME

Artistic expression *and* immediate gratification—what more could a kid ask for? Drop into this paint-your-own-ceramics studio and create a spur-of-the-moment masterpiece. You can prime it, paint it, finish it, and, with no kiln-baking required, take it home the same day.

Budding artists pick from hundreds of pre-molded plaster sculptures, from the somewhat useless (animal statues and plaques) to the less cluttering (bookends, trinket boxes, pencil holders, and picture frames). Prices (and level of difficulty) are designated by shelf color; the red shelf is the cheapest ($7.99 each), purple the most expensive ($23.99). Of course you'll want to steer kids away from the individually priced items, such as the full-size columns ($90) and the 3-foot gargoyle ($200).

Once the piece is chosen (the most daunting part for kids), it's on to paint and brush. Ultra-friendly staff can be counted on for amiable coaching throughout the process, right from tying on the smocks (the rule is: no smock, no painting) to "fairy" dusting the finished

KEEP IN MIND: The Dedham store is the latest of five Plaster Fun Time locations. Others are in Natick (251 W. Central St., tel. 508/651–7673), Redding (347 Main St., tel. 781/944–6383), Salem (400 Highland Ave., tel. 978/745–7788), and Newton (118 Needham St., Newton Highlands, tel. 617/244–6080). Be sure to wear old clothes, as paint is likely to stain. Repeat customers should ask about "Frequent Painter" cards, which offer a free piece after you've paid for 12. This place is an absolute lifesaver during school vacations (when there are extended hours) and inclement weather!

691 Providence Hwy.
(Rte. 1 southbound), Dedham

781/326–4445

$7.99 and up

M–F 11–7, Sa 10–7, Su 12–6

5–12

product. Parents of little perfectionists will be happy to know that pre-dry mistakes can be instantly washed away. On the other hand, owner Nancy Selvaggi begs grown-ups to keep their hands off. "The whole idea is to let the kids be the creators," she says. Over-zealous "helpers"—and we know who we are!—are best advised to get their own project. The final touch is a professionally applied spray that magically gives the piece a "baked" glow.

HEY, KIDS! The paint's dry, but it's not exactly as you'd envisioned. Don't despair! Ask about the magical wax coating that can bring out all kinds of neat features on your already dry work.

Prices include sculpture, primer, paints (as many colors as you want), and finish. The seemingly magical glitter (a secret in-house formula) is the hands-down favorite finishing touch. Lest anyone mistake this for a girls-only haven, check out the large supply of dinosaurs, skeletons, and swords, which has made art lovers out of many boys. Count on artists of both sexes to glow with pride over their newly minted creations.

KID-FRIENDLY EATS: It's not exactly the hometown institution implied by the name, but **Joe's American Bar & Grill** (985 Providence Hwy., tel. 781/329–0800) has a warm, cordial atmosphere and dishes to suit every taste, including the staples (ravioli and chicken fingers) on a vast children's menu. If you're heading north, you can't beat **Bertucci's** (683 VFW Pkwy., West Roxbury, tel. 617/327–0898) for great pizza and pasta. Also see Archery USA.

PLIMOTH PLANTATION

The year is 1627; the place is Plymouth, Massachusetts; and the townspeople are English settlers just arrived from the motherland. Just as those old historical films used to say, "You are there." Plimoth Plantation is a particularly engaging snippet of living history. What you'll find here is a re-creation of day-to-day village life in the early 17th century, complete with thatched-roof homes (there are about 20 buildings in total), period tools, and conservatively clad Pilgrims.

"Residents," in fact, are what make this experience so enjoyable. The town's inhabitants actually represent real people, whose stories are drawn from long-ago diaries, transcripts, and letters. Researchers went as far as to travel to England to study their subjects' roots. Costumed actors—adorned in surprisingly un-Pilgrim-like garb (in other words, no black hats and buckled shoes)—play their roles with aplomb, rarely, if ever, veering from their parts. You'll have to listen carefully to understand them, however; as with the characters themselves, accents and dialects are carefully honed. And you'll have to choose your

HEY, KIDS!

Do the Pilgrims' brand of livestock look a bit different than what you're used to? Farm animals here have been carefully bred to maintain their 17th-century appearance. One good example: All cows on the plantation, including the females, have horns.

KID-FRIENDLY EATS: Experience the tastes of traditional Pilgrim living at one of the daily luncheons; reservations can be made on your way into the visitor center. The Mexican food at **Sam Diego's** (51 Main St., tel. 508/747–0048) is on the standard side, but the old firehouse it's in makes it something special. Outstanding comfort food, such as meat loaf and pork chops, has made the **Colonial** (39 Main St., tel. 508/746–0838) a hometown favorite, though it's closed on Thursday. Look for lots of seafood shacks a short walk away from the *Mayflower*.

137 Warren Ave.
(Rte. 3 Exit 4), Plymouth

 508/746-1622

 $17 ages 13 and up,
$9.50 children 6–12

 Apr–late Nov, daily 9–5

All ages

words carefully to get directions to the bathroom; however, Pilgrims *will* take mercy on children doing the I-have-to-go-now dance.

English settlers aren't the only ones in town. At a nearby village dedicated to the Wampanoags, actual native people, dressed in traditional 17th-century native wear, answer questions about their people then and now.

The plantation is both fun and educational, and the Pilgrims manage to dispel a few myths along the way. Contrary to popular impression, settlers weren't all a somber lot. Oh, there were the stoic among them, but just as in today's world, the grim reapers were balanced by more boisterous folks. It may take a while to get into the 17th-century groove, and children may at first be taken aback by such greetings as "What cheer children? Have you come to help me in my labors?" But the rewards of interacting with people so well versed in this period of history, and so adept at making it interesting, are many.

KEEP IN MIND: While at the plantation, visit the *Mayflower II*, a replica with costumed interpreters. The cost is $7 ages 13 and up, $4.50 children 6–12, and combination tickets with Plimoth Plantation are available. For a grand tour of the rest of the area, including that famous slab of history, Plymouth Rock, check out the Plymouth Rock Trolley Company (tel. 508/747–3419). Its 40-minute narrated excursions allow you to get off and on at the different sites.

PRUDENTIAL CENTER SKYWALK

One of Boston's most famous skyscrapers isn't exactly known for its beauty. Built in 1965, the Prudential is widely considered a blot on the Boston skyline. ("It's exterior looks like a car radiator," commented one local architect.) But like Furbys and trolls, the Prudential building—or the Pru, as it's known to locals—seems to have turned its very homeliness into one of the things that makes it so loveable. And the really good news is that if you're inside looking out, you don't have to see it at all.

Though it's relinquished its title as the city's tallest—that honor now belongs to the John Hancock Tower (*see above*)—the building nevertheless boasts some pretty remarkable views. In fact, unlike the Hancock, whose southern exposure is closed to the public, the Pru offers vistas in all directions. Zoom up the elevator to the 50th floor, and you'll be surrounded by a panorama of the city and beyond. On a clear day, you can see all the way to Cape Cod. Low-key features accompanying the view include window graphics mapping out visible landmarks and several interesting displays that detail the city's past and present.

KEEP IN MIND: Since the Prudential doesn't provide brochures, bring a map to help you find your way around the view. Among the important landmarks you might see are Mt. Washington (the Northeast's tallest peak), to the north, and the tip of Cape Cod (Provincetown), to the southeast. To avoid confusing some of the Harbor Islands with Provincetown, look for the neck that connects it to the mainland. There are some pretty good views on the bottom floor, too, namely the store windows of the Pru's trendy shops (tel. 617/267–1002). Do yourself a favor and leave the credit cards at home.

800 Boylston St.

617/859-0648

 $4 ages 11 and up,
$3 children 3–10

 M–F 8:30–6, Sa 10–6, Su 11:30–6

5 and up

The Pru doesn't overtly embrace its status as a tourist attraction, a couple of coin-operated photo booths notwithstanding. There is nary a brochure to be found, and window graphics are a mite faded. But the subdued aura isn't necessarily a bad thing. Here, unlike at the Hancock Tower, you can actually get close enough to the windows to press your nose to the glass (theoretically, please—window washers hate that!). There are a couple of chairs sprinkled around, but inside window ledges make perfect window seats to sit peacefully and appreciate the view—almost like a visit to grandma's apartment. That the heating vents are mounted along these same ledges make them particularly warm, cozy spots for a winter's day.

HEY, KIDS! Question: Which bridge out there is the "Salt and Pepper Bridge?" Answer: The Longfellow Bridge. Look closely. It's capped by structures that resemble the little condiment holders on your dining room table.

KID-FRIENDLY EATS: The international flair of **Restaurant Marché Mövenpick** (tel. 617/578–700), located right in the Prudential shops, is an adventure all by itself. Your choices include pasta, pizza, chicken, and just about anything else you can think of—all cooked right in front of you. The marketplace also has a vast food court featuring, among other things, **Rebecca's** (tel. 617/266–3355), a café known for its tasty sandwiches and salads. This is an office building, however, and the court gets extremely busy during business lunch hours.

PUPPET SHOWPLACE THEATRE

Y ou'd think that such a low-tech diversion might fizzle when up against today's whiz-bang attractions. Not a chance. Though merchants have come and gone all around it, this little puppet-show-that-could has managed to hold its own despite the arrival of the high-tech generation.

Hiding behind a tiny storefront across from the Brookline Village T stop (blink and you could miss it), Puppet Showplace has been entertaining families for more than 25 years. No small-time sock-puppet organization here, this nonprofit group is professional through and through. In addition to staging its own performances, the company hosts regular appearances by renowned puppeteers from all over the world. Over the years, guest artists have presented ethnic folk tales and original stories as well as stalwarts such as *Cinderella*. Puppet Showplace owner/artistic director Paul Vincent Davis is an internationally regarded puppet master himself. He's known for his takes on classics, including *Rumplestilskin* and *Beauty and the Beast,* and has been lauded for adapting folklore, such as his "Raccoon Tales," adapted from stories of the Seneca Native American tribes.

KID-FRIENDLY EATS: Checkered tablecloths and huge portions of messy food are the order of the day at the **Village Smokehouse** (6–9 Harvard Sq., tel. 617/566–3782). The neighborhood hangout is right around the corner from the puppet theater (no, this is not the Harvard Square in Cambridge). Apart from the food, half the fun is watching the eats get cooked up center stage in the open pit. If barbecue doesn't suit your fancy, walk across the street from the theater for pizza and such at **Bertucci's** (4 Brookline Pl., tel. 617/731–2300).

32 Station St., Brookline

 $8

 Late May–Aug, M–F varying times; Sept–late May, Th 10:30, Sa–Su 1 and 3

 5 and up; Tot Th 3–5

617/731-6400

The Puppet Showplace organization prides itself on presenting colorful, nonthreatening fare. However, large (sometimes very large) puppets—occasionally 3 or 4 feet tall—can startle little ones. Ever aware of this potential "fear" factor (particularly during Tot Thursday performances), puppeteers often introduce themselves before stepping behind the stage, and many come out again after the show to allow kids a closer look at the "cast." Shows last about 45 minutes. Most "performers" are hand puppets; however, the theater does host the occasional marionette troupe. Stick around for the Make It and Take It workshops after some performances, and you may just get to create a puppet of your own.

KEEP IN MIND: Daily shows are often given during schools' winter vacations, but show frequency diminishes dramatically in the summer. Because of its small size (95 seats), Puppet Showplace is frequently a sellout, so call for reservations. Since seating is unreserved, arrive early for the best choice, though there really isn't a bad seat in the house. After-show workshops are held after most, but not all, 3 o'clock weekend performances (reservations required). The cost is $8 per puppet, meaning that mom and dad don't have to pay to come and help.

PURGATORY CHASM

It's only fitting that a place called purgatory should take you on a jagged path progressively downward. But despite its ominous moniker, this natural wonder is actually a slice of adventure heaven, a place accurately described by local rangers as a natural playground for kids. You'll travel about an hour from Boston to get here, but it's definitely worth the trip.

A find dating back to the 18th century, the place got its name from the spooky aura created by towering rocks and thick, unwieldy brush (since removed by rangers). As for the origin of the chasm itself, experts are still debating it. An 18th-century villager swore it opened up overnight, but more scientific theories attribute it to earthquakes and glaciers.

On paper, the ¼-mile-long, 50-foot-wide chasm doesn't seem so vast. Inside is another story. Huge, craggy rocks jut out in all directions, requiring nimble feet—and unfettered hands—to navigate. The circuit is most definitely a challenge, and you'll need to be physically fit (not to mention non-claustrophobic) to manage it. But don't be deterred by the

HEY, KIDS! A lot of the chasm's landmarks have spooky names. Devil's Coffin, an above-ground cave you can actually go in, has a large, rectangular stone that looks like a vampire's coffin. Mother Nature even saw fit to include what looks like a headstone. Be sure to look for the old verse carved at the entrance: "Prepare to meet thy God." It looks to have been carved about 100 years ago, but no one knows its exact origins.

198 Purgatory Rd.
(I–90 to Rte. 146S), Sutton

508/234-3733 or
508/234-9610

Free

Daily sunrise–sunset

5 and up

beginning. Those first few steps are indeed some doozies, necessitating a little hands-and-knees maneuvering. But once you get past the Devil's Pulpit (those Puritans just loved those bedeviled titles), the going gets easier. The most popular trail takes you 1½ miles to the bottom of the chasm (70 feet down) and back; look for the blue paint that marks the trail. Take a hard left at Devil's Coffin or you'll veer off the rocks onto a rather ordinary wooded path. (A note to the adventurous and foolhardy: Climbing the surrounding rock faces is strictly prohibited without a permit.) The faint of heart (and not everyone will feel comfortable climbing here) can still enjoy the view on the trails that run the chasm's perimeter. Skip the trails entirely in winter and wet weather, when slippery conditions make them unsafe. The 110-acre park also includes a picnic area, playground equipment, and, perhaps best of all, a shiny new visitor center with shiny new bathrooms you can use after you're done communing with nature.

KID-FRIENDLY EATS: Picnic in the gazebo at the trailhead, where an ice cream truck parks in summer. For more ice cream (40 varieties), hot dogs, soups, and snacks, cross Route 146 to **West End Creamery** (481 Purgatory Rd., Whitinsville, tel. 508/234-2022). **Blue Jay's** (489 Central Tpke., Wilkinsonville, tel. 508/865-9955) serves comfort food.

KEEP IN MIND: Remember three words: Bring bandage strips. Though most kids manage the terrain with ease (and better than their parents), scrapes happen. You'll kick yourself if you're at the bottom of the chasm with a boo-booed, crying child. A bottle of water isn't a bad idea, either. Food, on the other hand, is prohibited in the chasm. Whatever you carry, put it in a backpack, because you'll need your hands to climb. And since it's 10° cooler at the bottom, bring a sweatshirt, although you're bound to work up a sweat on the climb.

SALEM

No allusion to the American witch is complete without a reference to Salem. The quiet, seaside enclave was seemingly brimming with dark artists a few centuries ago. Back then, scads of young women were accused of practicing witchcraft, which led to the infamous Salem Witch Trials and made the town the best-known horror hamlet this side of Transylvania.

A surprise to most kids, the witches here have nothing to do with pointed black hats or twitching noses, a fact illustrated at the Salem Witch Museum (Washington Sq., tel. 978/744–1692). A good place to become oriented, the museum describes what really started the hysteria—basically an overreaction to teenage-girl rebellion—and how it led to the hangings of 19 of the accused. The Witch Dungeon Museum (16 Lunde St., tel. 978/741–3570) goes a few steps further, guiding visitors through its dungeons and re-creating the trial of Sarah Good. You can even "enjoy" the sight of the reconstructed gallows. Figurines (some of them grim) at the Salem Wax Museum (288 Derby St., tel. 978/298–2929) depict wayward seafarers as well as witches. The short tour of Nathaniel Hawthorne's House of Seven Gables (54 Turner St., tel. 978/744–0991) is mostly architectural, but a trip

HEY, KIDS!
The secret staircase in the House of Seven Gables is famous for hiding not witches, but slaves. Before slavery was abolished in this country, the stairwell—which became hidden after an 18th-century addition was put on the original house—was used as an escape passage in the Underground Railway.

KEEP IN MIND: Salem has more to offer than witchcraft. See maritime history at the Salem Maritime National Historic Site (174 Derby St., tel. 978/740–1660). Ne'er-do-wells of the sea are explored at the New England Pirate Museum (274 Derby St., tel. 978/741–2800). Life in 1630s Salem is re-created at Pioneer Village (Forest River Park, tel. 978/744–0991). Two centuries of art and artifacts are on display at the Peabody Essex Museum (East India Sq., tel. 978/745–4054), and for a grand tour by land and sea, try Moby Duck (New Liberty St., tel. 978/741–4386).

up the secret staircase where young girls accused of witchery were once hidden (it's narrow, folks, so suck in your guts) will no doubt be a thrill. Learn about the practice of real witchcraft at Salem Witch Village (282 R. Derby St., tel. 800/298–2929).

That Salem has embraced its mystical image is evidenced by such attractions as the Museum of Myths and Monsters (59 Wharf St., tel. 978/745–7283). The ghouls inside have absolutely nothing to do with Colonial-era witches, but they do fit in with the creepy theme. The town becomes particularly magical in October, when haunted happenings include spooky houses, street fairs, and concerts (some events may be too scary for some kids). Call the Salem Halloween Committee (tel. 978/744–0013) for information.

KID-FRIENDLY EATS: The name may not sound hospitable, but **In a Pig's Eye** (148 Derby St., tel. 978/741–4436) serves renowned sandwiches, salads, and pastas, plus a few Mexican specialties. Make sure to save room for dessert! For a scenic meal, head down to **Victoria Station** (Pickering Wharf, tel. 978/745–3400), where an enormous menu of burgers, salads, and such takes second place to the water view.

SIX FLAGS NEW ENGLAND

You've got to hand it to Six Flags for their scare-the-pants-off-of-you contraptions. Roller coaster enthusiasts, start your engines: This new ride emporium is rife with the stuff of thrill seekers' dreams.

Formerly the family-owned Riverside Amusement Park, this Massachusetts staple shed its mom-and-pop roots in 1996, when it was purchased by Premier Parks. Today the banner reads Six Flags (Premier Parks bought the mega-park operator), and the park now has name recognition and all the bells and whistles—and cartoon characters—to go with it.

Six Flags is known for its constitution-challenging assortment of rides, and the offerings here seem right in character. Like scary? Try Flashback, a high-speed jaunt that takes you turning and looping one way, and then does it all again—backwards. Then soar with the Man of Steel at speeds of up to 70 miles per hour on Superman—Ride of Steel. At 2½ minutes, this baby is l-o-o-ng by roller coaster standards, screaming out of the starting gate with a 221-foot drop. It's New England's tallest, fastest, and longest coaster and is

KID-FRIENDLY EATS: If you haven't lost your lunch on Superman (or if you have and you need to fill 'er up again), try the **Superhero Grill,** which has the requisite burgers and fries. In Movie Town, the **Commissary** has reasonably priced burgers and chicken—a big plate will run about $6, but the drink will tack on another $2—atop an enormous mound of fries, which may or may not be a good thing. Right across the street from the water park, **Cooks in the Kitchen** (1668 Main St., tel. 413/786–8068) offers burgers, sandwiches, fish-and-chips—and air conditioning!

1623 Main St., Agawam

413/786-9300

 $34.99 48" and up,
$17.49 36"–47"

 Late Apr–late May and early Sept–Oct, Sa–Su 10–9; Memorial Day–Labor Day, daily 10–10

 All ages

the focal point of a new 12-acre park section including such groovy restaurants as the DC Comics Diner (hint: eat after you ride). If all of this doesn't leave you a quivering hunk of mush, try out Scream, another of the self-explanatory monster thrill rides that have jump-started the park's transformation.

Thankfully, Six Flags has taken mercy on the less iron-gutted among us, offering lower-thrill fare as well. Poison Ivy's Twisted Train, for example, is billed as a family coaster. If you need to remove yourself from the big guns completely, try Looney Tunes Movie Town, a family area featuring rides and shows, as well as that Wascally Wabbit (AKA Bugs Bunny) and friends.

KEEP IN MIND:
Since Six Flags is new, expect crowds through summer 2001. Dress appropriately in summer, as the cement landscape gets mighty hot and only one restaurant is air-conditioned! To cool off, bring a swimsuit and visit the adjacent Island Kingdom water park (included in price). Discounted admission is offered after 4.

TRANSPORTATION: Though the directions aren't nearly as complicated as they may seem, make sure you have a copy with you. Take I-90 west to Exit 6, I-291 west. Travel 4.2 miles to I-91 south. Travel 2.8 miles to Exit 3. Cross the bridge and take the first exit. Follow the rotary to Route 57 west, then to Route 159 south, which is Main Street. Six Flags is 2.9 miles down on the left. Getting here will take a good 1½ hours, but that's better than a three-hour flight to a national theme park.

SOUTHWICK'S ZOO

What do you do when you're an animal conservationist with a dairy farm? Sell the cattle and turn the place into a zoo. That's just what Justin Southwick did in 1952, transforming his 200-year-old homestead into a home for animals large and small. Today Southwick's has evolved into a full-fledged private zoo—purportedly New England's largest—with lions, tigers, bears, and all. There are about 500 unlikely beasts here, some endangered, some just plain cute. Though purists once balked at some of the smaller habitats (a result of the facility's 1950s origins), the zoo has recently taken great pains to bring their structures up-to-date (among the newest additions are lion and tiger habitats), and there's no question that Southwick's animals are well loved.

Close encounters are what set Southwick's apart. Animals here are accessible (the aforementioned lions, tigers, and bears notwithstanding). Giraffes are so close, you can almost look them in the eye—if, of course, they were to bend down over their fence, which they sometimes do. Elephants stand close enough for you to see how hairy they really are. For an extra charge, you can actually ride one of the big guys; the zoo

HEY, KIDS!

The giraffe duo here are a mom and dad, Uno and Dos. (Their little baby—Tres, natch—is off visiting friends in another zoo.) Some of the other creative names you'll find here include Bonnie and Clyde, the rhinos.

KID-FRIENDLY EATS: With cozy benches and booths, homespun **Lowell's** (16 Hastings St., tel. 508/473–1073) looks positively old-time, and has comfort food to match. The enormous menu of sandwiches, salads, and seafood—even a "rooster" (fresh fried chicken) for kids should have something to please everyone. **New England Steak and Seafood** (11 Uxbridge Rd. [Rte. 16], tel. 508/473–5079) has a similarly vast menu but in a more formal, but still comfortable, atmosphere. Choices include pasta, seafood, and grills, as well as a large children's menu. The zoo itself has a couple of snack shacks.

2 Southwick St. (off Rte.16), Mendon

 May–Columbus Day, daily 10–5; limited operation Apr and late Oct

 $12 ages 13 and up, $8 children 3–12

508/883–9182 or 800/258-9182

 All ages

offers camel and pony rides as well (weight restrictions apply for these). In the petting zoo, goats and sheep including absolutely adorable kids and lambs—are more than happy to accept offerings of food from your kids and lambs (use the feed machines only, please). Don't bother trying to hide the pellets; these hungry hogs (figuratively speaking) will nibble right out of your pocket!

One of the zoo's most unusual features and a definite highlight is the Deer Forest. Dozens of deer call this 35-acre, gated forest home. Grab a 25¢ fistful of feed from one of the machines and enjoy as the deer nibble directly from your hand. You could spend the better part of the day right here. After the animal adventures, go wild at the on-site playground or on the small collection of kiddie rides.

KEEP IN MIND: Animal feeding is a wonderful thing as long as you're aware of the creatures' dispositions. Friendly (and hungry!) deer sometimes swarm food-toting visitors, a circumstance that, while not dangerous, can be frightening to a young child. Ask for a schedule of daily presentations about elephants, primates, and reptiles.

SWAN BOATS AT THE PUBLIC GARDEN

You know it's spring in Boston when the swans come back to town. Not the real birds (although those are here, too), but the oversize floating entities known as the Swan Boats. Fixtures in Boston for more than 100 years, these graceful birds migrate back to the Public Garden each April, giving thousands of delighted passengers perfectly serene jaunts around the famous lagoon.

Set afloat in 1877 by entrepreneur Robert Paget, the watercraft have become a symbol of the complete Boston experience. Paget's idea was simply to provide a novel diversion. The concept for the swan came out of the need to camouflage the mechanism for locomotion, in this case a human-propelled paddle wheel. And talk about low-tech! Fifteen-minute lagoon tours are made possible only through the efforts of some very energetic crewmen (one per boat), who motor the 20-passenger vehicles by pedaling.

That the setting is the Public Garden makes the adventure all the more peaceful. Far more formal than its sibling (the Boston Common) across Charles Street, the manicured garden

KEEP IN MIND: Because they're operated by humans, the Swan Boats are docked during especially rainy, windy, and hot days. Look for the real (feathered) swans to arrive back at the lagoon in late spring.

Public Garden,
Boston Common

 617/522–1966

Boats $2 ages 16 and
up, $1 children 2–15;
garden free

Mid-Apr–mid-June and early–mid-Sept, daily 10–4;
mid-June–early Sept, daily 10–5

All ages

is decidedly more of a keep-off-the-grass kind of place (don't even think about bringing the Frisbee). Nevertheless, the 24-acre parcel, the nation's first public botanical garden, has its own charms, namely hundreds of species of flora. Well-marked paths pass by all of the prized plantings, and spring blooms make the garden a tapestry of color. All of that may well be lost on little ones, who would just as soon make a beeline to that homage to mallard-dom, the Duckling Sculpture. Bronze casts commemorate the fictional exploits of the *Make Way for Ducklings* clan (*see above*). Feel free to climb on them; just don't take them home. (Despite having their webbed feet sunk in cement, the quackers have been the occasional victims of duck-nappers).

HEY, KIDS! A few centuries ago, before dirt was carted in as fill, Boston was but a square mile surrounded by water. The blooming turf that is the Public Garden was a patch of salt marsh, and if you were where F.A.O. Schwarz now is, you'd have been swimming.

KID-FRIENDLY EATS: "Cheers" fans will recognize the exterior of the **Bull & Finch Pub** (84 Beacon St., tel. 617/227–9605) as the place where everybody knows your name. There's no Norm or Cliff, but there's plenty of above-average pub fare to fill you up. It is somewhat pricey, however; this is, after all, a tourist attraction. For another local suggestion, see the Boston Common.

TOT STOP

5

T hink of this as the mother of all indoor play places. Around for more then a decade (making it the oldest one in town), this well-stocked, friendly, and super-clean facility has endured by giving young children the thing they want most—lots of things to play with and plenty of room to do it in.

Begun by a mom, Tot Stop became a success because of its simple recipe: toys. While "interactive" has become the buzzword of fancy children's attractions, Tot Stop personifies the term without bells and whistles. As one manager asserts, the place features just about every plastic, wood, and foam plaything you might want to have in your own house but would never have the room for. Nearly 7,000 square feet is literally brimming with "totally kid-activated, non-coin-operated" toys, from blocks to dollhouses to music-makers, not to mention a whole fleet of foot-powered vehicles. A large infant area has age-appropriate toys, and there are numerous play structures (such as a giant barn) for climbing, sliding, and setting up house. You can even sun at the "beach," thanks to a giant sandpit complete with built-in aquarium.

KID-FRIENDLY EATS: The facility has a low-key **sandwich counter** that sells all the important kid food, such as grilled cheese, tuna sandwiches, and PB & Js. Best of all, you can avoid throwing away leftovers by ordering only a half sandwich. If you'd prefer to go out, grab a pizza or pasta at **Bertucci's** (5 Cambridge Park Dr., tel. 617/876–2200). Tot Stop allows you to leave for lunch and return without paying an additional fee.

Playthings aside, what parents seem to appreciate most is how easy it is to be here. Located in the auditorium of an old junior high school, Tot Stop has wide-open spaces that allow children to be seen from virtually anywhere in the room. That means parents can get some much-needed grown-up time while kids go to town on their own (remember, however, that you are absolutely responsible for watching your own child). On the flip side, all play areas are grown-up accessible, meaning you can actually join your kids at their pretend tea party or chase them through the small climbing tube. Thoughtful touches include safety-gated stairways and oversize windows that allow for lots of attitude-adjusting natural light. The place keeps its clean badge of honor with nightly scourings, during which even the pretend hard hats are disinfected and bleached.

KEEP IN MIND: The maximum family charge (for three or more siblings) is $13.95. Tot Stop gets busiest in the morning until about noon and then again around 3, ostensibly after nap time. You can save a few dollars by coming Friday after 5, when admission is reduced. Friday night is also pizza night; call in advance, and for an extra charge, you can have a pizza delivered when you arrive.

U.S.S. CONSTITUTION

Old Ironsides doesn't sound like a nickname befitting a lady, but then this is no ordinary lady. Boston's grande dame of the sea, the U.S.S. *Constitution* achieved fame—not to mention her sturdy nickname—during the War of 1812, when her thick skin reportedly deflected a cannonball fired by the British frigate H.M.S. *Guerriere*. Nearly 200 years later, the old girl is still alive and kicking, currently the oldest commissioned warship still afloat.

In 1997, the historic vessel set the nautical world abuzz when she hoisted anchor and sailed out of the harbor for the first time in more than 100 years. These days you're more likely to see her docked than set to sea.

Thirty-minute guided tours of the vessel are led by active navy personnel. The uniform of the day—white trousers, bloused shirt, and black neckerchief—is sported by the Officer of the Deck, adding to the effect as you tour two of the ship's lower decks and see how 19th-century sailors bunked, ate, slept, and went to war. It's pretty impressive when you realize that anywhere between 400 and 500 men shared these cramped quarters for 12

HEY, KIDS! Some of the youngest sailors aboard the *Constitution* were called "powder monkeys." These quick and agile crewmen—some as young as 8, but mostly young teens—carried gunpowder during battles, running from the ship's bottom (where the powder was stored) up several decks to the guns. Guns had to be reloaded after every firing. Not only was the job exhausting, it was dangerous. Since they were essential to artillery operation, powder monkeys were often the targets of enemy fire. Alas, if you were a boy who wanted to go to sea, this was the only job in town.

Charlestown Navy Yard, Charlestown

 Free

617/242-5670 ship,
617/426-1812 museum

 Museum May–Oct, daily 9–6; Nov–Apr, daily 10–5

All ages

months at a time. But then, as a guide points out, the ship was built for war, not for pleasure cruising.

To fully appreciate the ship's legacy, you'll want to stop by the Constitution Museum. The three-story structure details the life of the vessel and her men through artifacts, such as ship's logs, journals, and sailor gear. Kid-friendly highlights include some interactive devices through which 19th-century sailing gets a 21st-century twist. A ship's wheel, for example, is attached to a computer screen that lets you navigate into war position, and virtual ammunition can be fired from the barrel of a real cannon. Anyone who has wondered how they get ships into those little bottles can visit the model makers' studios and maybe try their hand at fashioning a model themselves. (Check with the front desk on your way in for studio times.)

KID-FRIENDLY EATS: In summer, the **Shipyard Galley** (Bldg. 10, Pier 1, tel. 617/241-5660), opposite the ship, serves burgers and snacks. **Tavern on the Water** (1 Pier 6, 8th St., tel. 617/242-8040) provides good food year-round—from broiled seafood and burgers to a large children's menu plus stellar spots for watching the ships.

KEEP IN MIND: Tours of the *Constitution* are conducted every day between 9:30 and 3:30, but you can walk the upper decks only after 3:30. The entire ship closes down 20 minutes before sunset. To complete your nautical experience, visit the U.S.S. *Cassin Young,* also in the Charlestown Navy Yard. In its heyday, the WWII destroyer packed anti-aircraft, anti-submarine, and anti-ship weaponry.

WALDEN POND

3

Don't even bother bringing the cell phone to this peaceable pond. It probably won't work, but even if it did, you'd be missing the whole point. Massachusetts's most famous pond, after all, is nothing if not a place to get away from it all.

Though the esteemed swimming hole is still a retreat, it isn't quite as secluded as it used to be. Visible from the main road, Walden Pond is just steps from the corner of Routes 2 and 126. Miraculously, though, when you're down at the water's edge, it feels sequestered just the same, somehow retaining the idyllic aura that inspired Henry David Thoreau to pen a book in its name.

Thoreau took up residence on the pond in 1845, on a lot owned by friend Ralph Waldo Emerson. Holed up for two years in his one-room cabin (a replica of which stands near the parking lot), the writer communed with nature and wrote, ultimately publishing his experiences in the 1854 book *Walden: or, Life in the Woods*. The preservation of Thoreau's beloved land has become a cause célèbre for some of today's luminaries.

KID-FRIENDLY EATS: Good, reasonably priced fare in this touristy neighborhood isn't an easy find. At **Papa Razzi** (768 Elm St., tel. 978/371–0030), you'll find pizzas, pastas, salads, and kid fare. The **Ninety-Nine Restaurant** (13 Commonwealth Ave., tel. 978/369–0300) has pages of burgers, salads, soups, and others.

KEEP IN MIND: Walden's inherent charms are the good news; its over-popularity is the bad. Balmy weather can bring tens of thousands here. In order to protect the environment, rangers keep a tight lid on capacity (1,000 people max), turning away carloads of disappointed wannabe swimmers. To ensure a spot on the sand, arrive early on those hot summer days. Pets, fires, and motorized watercraft are prohibited. The park offers seasonal activities, including children's crafts, story times, and tours. Look outside the Walden shop or call the main number for information.

Though myriad four-legged animals—squirrels, rabbits, chipmunks, among others—continue to inhabit the area, it's the two-legged creatures that keep the place hopping. The fresh, clear water attracts more than a half million recreators annually, who come to swim, boat, picnic, or just to soak up the sun and scenery. Hiking is a year-round pastime; a scenic path runs 1.8 miles around the pond, and there are a total of 411 acres in the entire Walden Pond State Reservation. Anglers are often up to their waders with rod and reel, and cross-country skiers take to the trails in winter. But despite all these visitors and all this activity, nobody has explained why such a big body of water—what looks like a lake to the untrained eye—is called a pond.

HEY, KIDS! Though Thoreau made it famous, Walden has a history that stretches back far before the author's days. Purportedly, the pond was formed 12,000 years ago by the last New England glacier, a thawing chunk of which broke off and melted into this 103-foot "kettle hole." How did the pond get its name? There are lots of theories, one of which has it that "Walden" is a consolidation of "walled in," which describes the ridges enclosing the pond. Then again, it's just a theory.

WESTON SKI TRACK

2

What to do with a snow-covered golf course during the dead of winter? How about turning it into a cross-country skiing center? A couple of entrepreneurs came up with this brilliant idea in 1975, harnessing the grounds of a public golf course and grooming it for cross-country skiers. While it's true that cross-country enthusiasts (those with their own equipment anyway) can ski for free virtually anywhere there's open space, what sets the Weston track apart is its conveniences. Groomed trails are a plus, especially for beginners. Snow-making machines operate from late November through February, ensuring at least a little rural activity even when Mother Nature isn't cooperating. Equipment rental is available right on site. And where else can a family of four experience skiing (skis included!) for just about $60?

Nearly 10 miles of trails cover the entire golf course, though the track gets significantly smaller when there's no natural snow on the ground (snow-making capabilities seem to be limited to the area nearest the lodge). Nevertheless, even then there's still plenty to be entertaining.

KEEP IN MIND: The golf-course terrain doesn't require a thick layer of snow, so don't count the place out just because you don't have a foot in your backyard. Just call ahead if you're wondering. Even in cold weather, you can work up a sweat, so to be comfortable throughout your adventure, dress in layers that can be easily removed and tied around your waist. To keep feet warm and dry while snowshoeing, wear a pair of durable, waterproof hiking boots. Those with extra gear to stow can bring a lock and use any of the lockers in the ski rental room.

200 Park Rd., Weston

781/891-6575

$11 ages 13 and up,
$6 children 6–12

 Dec–Feb or as snow permits, M–Th
10–9:30, F 10–8, Sa 9–8, Su 9–6

4 and up

Rental skis are stocked for kids as young as 3. Reasonably priced lessons are offered to those age 4 and up. If your tykes are too little to get around on their own two feet, you can rent a PULK (a gizmo that looks like a sled version of those three-wheeled trailers that attach to bicycles) and tow them along behind you. For something completely different, you can suit up the family in snowshoes, also available for rent.

The Weston's trails are relatively flat, so beginners need not worry about racing out of control. The more adventurous will find at least a few small hills. Veterans say the full circuit can be experienced in a couple of hours, but you may want to stick around. Night lights let you continue your adventure for several hours after sunset.

KID-FRIENDLY EATS: The on-site **café** offers the all-important hot chocolate as well as hot dogs, soup, and snacks. If you'd like to warm up with some pizza or pasta, try **Papa Razzi** (16 Washington St., Wellesley, tel. 781/235–4747).

HEY, KIDS! Think cross-country is a snooze? Think again. Traditional cross-country skiing (what's called classical skiing) isn't the only way to travel. The new wave is "skate skiing," a method named for its skatinglike motion. You'll move a bit faster and still get some exercise. To give it a go, ask for "skates" when you rent (they're slightly different from regular skis), and stick to the specially groomed runs next to the traditional cross-country tracks. By the way, both styles are contested at the Olympics, so if you practice really hard . . .

WOLF HOLLOW

Y ou wouldn't think an animal as seemingly common as a wolf could be endangered, but it is. Despite its familiar name, wolves have dwindled significantly in numbers (the result of early 20th-century efforts to save farm livestock) and are all but gone in 47 of the 50 states. Though the statistic pretty much negates the possibility of encountering a wolf in the wild, you'll get the next best thing at this unique, nonprofit animal habitat.

Dedicated entirely to educating people about wolves and how to preserve them, the facility gets visitors close to a pack in its natural habitat, providing a rare glimpse into the work-and-play life of these wild canines. The animals can be viewed from just outside a 1½-acre enclosure. From just a few feet away, you'll be able to appreciate the personalities and appearances of the 14-member pack: the bearlike good looks of Denali, the graying coat of Geniek, or perhaps even the underbite of Lakota. While you observe, staff members detail the habits of these regal creatures and point out the significance of their behaviors.

HEY, KIDS!

Wolf packs have a distinct pecking order, and humans are at the bottom of it. To approach the pack, owner Joni Soffron must show her respect by crouching and avoiding eye contact with the alpha female (Tee Bee). Otherwise she risks a reprimand: a stern stare and a grab.

KEEP IN MIND: Wolf puppies come into the world in the second week in May (though not every year), and the little guys begin making public appearances when they're about two weeks old. To stand any chance of seeing the small pups, plan your visit for late May or June. For another type of wildlife adventure, check out Crane Beach/Crane Wildlife Refuge (Argilla Rd., tel. 978/356–4351). The shallow waters and climbing rocks of Wingaersheek Beach (Gloucester, tel. 978/281–9790) are a family favorite.

Wolf packs, it turns out, aren't all that different from human families. Each pack has a mother and father (the alpha female and male), who are the leaders. Siblings engage in rivalry (Delia, for example, gets picked on by her sister Missy), and children and subordinates show their respect by bowing when a parent enters. (OK, so they're not exactly like humans.) Once grown, pack members are assigned a job, such as hunting or puppy sitting. Performing the appointed task is crucial, says Joni Soffron, owner (with her husband, Paul) of Wolf Hollow. "If you don't do your job," she says, "you get kicked out of the pack."

Hour-long programs end with a group howl. Staff members counsel you on the correct pitch. If you're on key, you just may get the wolves to howl back.

KID-FRIENDLY EATS: Locals say the **Clam Box** (246 High St., tel. 978/356-9707) has the best fried clams in the East; however, the restaurant is closed December through February. For a large selection of burgers, salads, and such, head to the popular **Choate Bridge Pub** (3 S. Main St., tel. 978/356-2931).

games

THE CLASSICS

"I'M THINKING OF AN ANIMAL..." With older kids you can play 20 Questions: Have your leader think of an animal, vegetable, or mineral (or, alternatively, a person, place, or thing) and let everybody else try to guess what it is. The correct guesser takes over as leader. If no one figures out the secret within 20 questions, the first person goes again. With younger children, limit the guessing to animals and don't put a ceiling on how many questions can be asked. With rivalrous siblings, just take turns being leader. Make the game's theme things you expect to see at your day's destination.

"I SEE SOMETHING YOU DON'T SEE AND IT IS BLUE." Stuck for a way to get your youngsters to settle down in a museum? Sit them down on a bench in the middle of a room and play this vintage favorite. The leader gives just one clue—the color—and everybody guesses away.

FUN WITH THE ALPHABET

"I'M GOING TO THE GROCERY..." The first player begins, "I'm going to the grocery and I'm going to buy... " and finishes the sentence with the name of an object, found in grocery stores, that begins with the letter "A". The second player repeats what the first player has said, and adds the name of another item that starts with "B". The third player repeats everything that has been said so far and adds something that begins with "C" and so on through the alphabet. Anyone who skips or misremembers an item is out (or decide up front that you'll give hints to all who need 'em). You can modify the theme depending on where you're going that day, as "I'm going to X and I'm going to see..."

"I'M GOING TO ASIA ON AN ANT TO ACT UP." Working their way through the alphabet, players concoct silly sentences stating where they're going, how they're traveling, and what they'll do.

FAMILY ARK Noah had his ark—here's your chance to build your own. It's easy: Just start naming animals and work your way through the alphabet, from antelope to zebra.

WHAT I SEE, FROM A TO Z In this game, kids look for objects in alphabetical order—first something whose name begins with "A", next an item whose name begins with "B", and so on. If you're in the car, have children do their spotting through their own window. Whoever gets to Z first wins. Or have each child play to beat his own time. Try this one as you make your way through zoos and museums, too.

JUMP-START A CONVERSATION

WHAT IF...? Riding in the car and waiting in a restaurant are great times to get to know your youngsters better. Begin with imaginative questions to prime the pump.

• If you were the tallest man on earth, what would your life be like? The shortest?
• If you had a magic carpet, where would you go? Why? What would you do there?
• If your parents gave you three wishes, what would they be?
• If you were elected president, what changes would you make?
• What animal would you like to be and what would your life be like?
• What's a friend? Who are your best friends? What do you like to do together?
• Describe a day in your life 10 years from now.

DRUTHERS How do your kids really feel about things? Just ask. "Would you rather eat worms or hamburgers? Hamburgers or candy?" Choose serious and silly topics—and have fun!

FAKER, FAKER Reveal three facts about yourself. The catch: One of the facts is a fake. Have your kids ferret out the fiction. Take turns being the faker. Fakers who stump everyone win.

KEEP A STRAIGHT FACE

"HA!" Work your way around the car. First person says "Ha." Second person says "Ha, ha." Third person says "Ha" three times. And so on. Just try to keep a straight face. Or substitute "Here, kitty, kitty, kitty!"

WIGGLE & GIGGLE Give your kids a chance to stick out their tongues at you. Start by making a face, then have the next person imitate you and add a gesture of his own—snapping fingers, winking, clapping, sneezing, or the like. The next person mimics the first two and adds a third gesture, and so on.

JUNIOR OPERA During a designated period of time, have your kids sing everything they want to say.

IGPAY ATINLAY Proclaim the next 30 minutes Pig Latin time, and everybody has to talk in this fun code. To speak it, move the first consonant of every word to the end of the word and add "ay." "Pig" becomes "igpay," and "Latin" becomes "atinlay." To words that being with a vowel, just add "ay" as a suffix.

MORE GOOD TIMES

BUILD A STORY "Once upon a time there lived..." Finish the sentence and ask the rest of your family, one at a time, to add another sentence or two. Bring a tape recorder along to record the narrative—and you can enjoy your creation again and again.

NOT THE GOOFY GAME Have one child name a category. (Some ideas: first names, last names, animals, countries, friends, feelings, foods, hot or cold things, clothing.) Then take turns naming things that fall into that category. You're out if you name something that doesn't belong in the category—or if you can't think of another item to name. When only one person remains, start again. Choose categories depending on where you're going or where you've been—historic topics if you've seen a historic sight, animal topics before or after the zoo, upside-down things if you've been to the circus, and so on. Make the game harder by choosing category items in A-B-C order.

COLOR OF THE DAY Choose a color at the beginning of your outing and have your kids be on the lookout for things that are that color, calling out what they've seen when they spot it. If you want to keep score, keep a running list or use a pen to mark points on your kids' hands for every item they spot.

CLICK If Cam Jansen, the heroine of a popular series of early-reader books, says "Click" as she looks at something, she can remember every detail of what she sees, like a camera (that's how she got her nickname). Say "Click!" Then give each one of your kids a full minute to study a page of a magazine. After everyone has had a turn, go around the car naming items from the page. Players who can't name an item or who make a mistake are out.

THE QUIET GAME Need a good giggle—or a moment of calm to figure out your route? The driver sets a time limit and everybody must be silent. The last person to make a sound wins.

THEMATIC INDEX

ACKNOWLEDGMENTS

A thousand thank-yous go to PR people all over the city, as well as the folks at the Boston Convention and Visitor's Bureau (Aimee O'Brien: you're a life-saver!) and to Boston Park Ranger Emily Prigot, who got me up to speed on my Boston history. My thanks to Nancy Holland, Jennifer Moore, Kim Repella, and all of my favorite "road testers" at the Burke and McGovern schools: Ashly, Kaitlyn, Chelsea, Alexander, Nicholas, Julia, Emma, Sarah, Jennifer, Richard, Rachel, Gregory, Matthew, Joseph, Joshua, Adria, Emily, Brittany, Shauna, Christina, Ryan, Brian, Eric, Andrew, John, Derek, Taylor, Curtis, Casey, Anthony, Nicholas, William, Andrew, Thomas, Matthew, Caitlin, Michael, Alison, Katherine, Brian, Katherine, Aaron, Tyler, Matthew, Kimberley, Alaina, Steven, and Nathan. Thanks to all the Medway moms who shared their great ideas—especially those at the Cedar Farms bus stop. My undying gratitude to my patient, wise, and eternally good-humored editor, Andrea Lehman. And finally, to my family—Steve, Alexis, and Melissa—who let me drag them around on endless escapades, I wouldn't have missed a minute.

—Lisa Oppenheimer